2020 VISION

Graham White is a former journalist and news executive who was assistant editor of *The Herald* in Melbourne before establishing his own public affairs consultancy. He provided advice to major Australian and multinational companies, industry associations, professional bodies, federal government agencies and environmental groups before retiring in 1999 to concentrate on writing and research. He has since assisted with studies into the characteristics of innovative businesses in Australia and industry perceptions of the effectiveness of R and D incentives. He lives outside Melbourne.

2020 VISION

HOW GLOBAL BUSINESS LEADERS SEE AUSTRALIA'S FUTURE

GRAHAM WHITE

ALLEN & UNWIN

First published in 2003

Allen & Unwin
83 Alexander Street
Crows Nest NSW 2065
Australia
Phone: (61 2) 8425 0100
Fax: (61 2) 9906 2218
Email: info@allenandunwin.com
Web: www.allenandunwin.com

National Library of Australia
Cataloguing-in-Publication entry:

White, Graham, 1939–.
2020 vision: how our global business leaders
see Australia's future.
ISBN 1 74114 002 1.
1. Economic forecasting – Australia. 2. Social prediction – Australia. 3. Globalization. 4. Chief executive officers – Australia – Interviews. 5. Australia – Economic conditions – 21st century. 6. Australia - Social conditions - 21st century. I. Title. II. Title: Twenty twenty vision.

330.99407

Cover, text design and typesetting by Studio Pazzo
Printed by Griffin Press, South Australia

10 9 8 7 6 5 4 3 2 1

CONTENTS

Introduction

In this book six internationally eminent Australians, leaders in their fields of industry and science, offer their views on the outlook for Australia and Australians.

It was not a task for which they volunteered: some required a degree of arm twisting — protesting that as their jobs require them to live abroad, they did not want to be seen offering gratuitous advice to a country where they no longer reside. However, once persuaded that they could make a contribution, each put in significant effort to be thoughtful and objective.

They were also generous with their time. It is probably true that time is always a CEO's most precious commodity, but circumstances conspired to make it even more so for several of them.

Jac Nasser was in the throes of an internal battle at Ford — one that ultimately cost him his job — when I visited him at the company's global headquarters outside Detroit. It was undoubtedly the most critical moment in his professional life, but had it not been for the TV crews hovering in the foyer below, you would never have known it: Nasser talked of Australia for over an hour with a passion and single-mindedness that belied the circumstances. Then he put on his jacket and went down to face the media. It was a virtuoso performance.

Similarly, Rod Eddington conducted an interview some months after the September 11 terrorist attacks — when airline business confidence was plummeting and British Airways, like all other major airlines, was haemorrhaging cash. 'Crisis' was the word of the day in media headlines. Again, it must have taken a Herculean effort for him to focus on the less urgent matter of Australia's future, while his company's own future was so precarious, but he did so with infectious enthusiasm. At the end of the discussion he left for a meeting at the Houses of Parliament in Westminster. No prizes for guessing what might have been on the agenda there.

For Rupert Murdoch, there was a double distraction. He was in the middle of a multi-billion dollar takeover deal and a crucial meeting with the other party had delayed the start of our interview. The meeting hadn't gone well, he confided. Then, perhaps 40 minutes later, his PA interrupted our discussions to suggest there was a call on the line that he might like to take. Takeover discussions were resumed. At the conclusion of the call, Murdoch needed less than a minute to regroup his thoughts and continue our discussion. Back on track, you could have believed he had nothing but Australia's future on his mind

Compounding this, it was a bad day on Wall Street. As we talked a TV monitor on the wall behind Murdoch silently chronicled the slide in the Dow Jones index — and with it the value of News Corporation shares (and Murdoch's private wealth). The screen was directly in my line of vision. Noting my distracted glance, he turned, watched for a moment, then said calmly: 'It's not looking good, is it?' Then he resumed talking about Australia.

Lord May was forced to interrupt our discussions to take a lengthy call from Britain's Science Minister. He too picked up the threads of the interview without missing a beat.

These vignettes tell us three things about the interviewees. First, that they are great actors (or poker players). If such events troubled or distracted them — as they must have done — the executives gave no clue.

Second, they have a great ability to concentrate; to switch from one topic to another and give each topic in turn the undivided attention of their obviously keen minds.

Third — and perhaps most important — these incidents reveal the amount of thought that all six have obviously given over the years to the issue of Australia and its future. Such distractions and pressures at the time of the interviews meant they had had little opportunity to rehearse their views beforehand and even less opportunity to develop them as we talked. Therefore the coherence of their analysis and the extent of knowledge that framed each discussion suggests they have given a lot of thought to these questions over a long time. Despite their global ambitions and responsibilities, these high-flyers appear to remain Australian at heart. Australia's future is still an issue that engages their minds.

Notwithstanding that proof of their sincerity, the question needs to be asked: why should we be interested in what six affluent Australians now mostly living abroad think about the outlook for our country?

The answer: because they are better placed to form such views than most of us, including many who commentate more regularly on these things.

That's not necessarily because they are smarter — though one is inclined to think that anybody who makes it to global leadership in their field probably has something going for them — but because it is their business to know. They also have access to information to which the rest of us are not privy.

When you are running the global businesses of Ford or Philip Morris you can directly compare the productivity of workers in Australia, Korea, Europe or the US. When you are making long-term investment decisions that may run into billions of dollars you analyse very carefully the economic and political prospects of the host country. You weigh the prospects of one against another. You weigh all aspects of the society.

If you are a genuine top-ranking figure — as all six are — you also get exposed to new ideas. You talk with other global leaders, both commercial and political. You have your own R&D departments, your own strategic development analysts, your own economists. You can sponsor think tanks and commission studies. You survive and prosper by getting right those big decisions about which countries will have the highest market growth or the best investment potential. You also survive by understanding the impacts of technology or of trade negotiations, and that can frequently mean discussing the issues directly with government ministers. You have that sort of access.

If you are Robert May you can access teams of experts to make objective comparisons of the cost-effectiveness of various national scientific programs. Your reputation is built on being able to draw the right conclusions from the data.

It goes without saying that the six Australians who participated in this project not only have access to such information, but are themselves remarkable individuals.

Geoff Bible, Leigh Clifford and Jacques Nasser all worked their way up from modest positions in the outposts of their global companies to the CEO's chair in the US or UK. Geoff Bible, who stepped down in late 2002, made it not just to CEO, but also President of Philip Morris and of associated company Kraft. When outsiders from the very fringes of these commercial empires can storm the citadels in this way you have to assume they are extraordinarily good at what they do.

Rod Eddington did not have to work his way to the top of

British Airways. After successfully running airlines in Australia and Asia, he was head-hunted to take over the reins of 'the world's favourite airline'. That speaks for itself.

Rupert Murdoch wasn't invited into the inner sanctum; he forced his way in. Inheriting the family shareholding of a small evening newspaper in Adelaide, he built it — through management flair and commercial boldness — into one of the world's great media empires. Today News Corporation controls newspapers in the US, UK, Australia and Asia, TV networks across Asia, Europe, the US and Australia, a major film studio and book and magazine publishing divisions. He is, by anybody's reckoning, a global media force.

Robert May — now Lord May of Oxford — took another route altogether. A Sydney university graduate, he won, by sheer force of his intellect, professorships at some of the world's most prestigious universities, including Princeton in the US and Oxford in Britain. His reputation is such that his scientific peers elected him president of Britain's Royal Society, one of the world's oldest and most respected scientific bodies. Prime Minister Tony Blair appointed him Britain's Chief Scientific Adviser and in that role he developed a blueprint to ensure that British researchers and British industry are at the forefront in a world where knowledge and technology are emerging as prime currencies. What is most remarkable in all this is that Lord May himself is not from one of the commercially exciting branches of science like biotechnology or information technology. His doctorate was in theoretical physics, but much of his more recent work has had an environmental bent.

So, the six participants are worth listening to just on the basis of their own demonstrated capacities and the access they have to knowledge about global patterns. But there is a further, equally persuasive reason to seek their views. By good fortune, their areas of direct expertise also parallel those which are likely to influence Australia's place in the world of the mid-twenty-first century.

Think of issues that might affect our future. Science and technology and the way it is transforming the nature of wealth and the nature of work: who better to understand its impact than Lord May, President of the Royal Society and architect of Britain's policies on these very issues? Or Leigh Clifford — because Rio Tinto conducts much of its global research in Australia and Clifford's own head of research, Dr Robin Batterham, is also Australia's chief scientific adviser. Or Rupert Murdoch who has not merely participated in the world's communications revolution but who, through his global networks of satellite and cable TV, has been one of its drivers.

Then there is the issue of globalisation: is any company more global than the Philip Morris Group that Geoff Bible headed? The world's greatest provider of packaged consumer goods operates on every continent producing and marketing tobacco products, dairy foods, confectionery, coffee, beer and a host of other products. And there is Jac Nasser, who at Ford not only commanded Ford's own global development, manufacturing and marketing networks but had equal access to the comparative performance of companies such as Jaguar, Volvo and Mazda which Ford either owns or has a substantial holding in. And, of course, Rupert Murdoch's interests likewise span the US, Europe, Asia and Australia. He is one of the most global thinkers in world business.

There's the question of our relations with Asia. Rod Eddington lived and worked in Asia for sixteen years. He ran one of Asia's most successful airlines, married there and now runs a global airline which has routes there. Rupert Murdoch operates Asia's most extensive TV network. Ford has interests in both Japan and Korea and Philip Morris has businesses throughout the entire continent. Leigh Clifford has his own special interest: East Asia is the biggest market for Rio Tinto's Australian-produced iron and coal. All of these interests cause the participants to track Asia's social and political trends as well as its economic growth and to stay in touch with government figures there.

It becomes hard to think of six individuals from any background who are more attuned to the issues that are central to Australia.

The six participants in this project may be perfectly matched for their roles, but they are certainly not the only internationally eminent Australian business leaders who might have contributed. Douglas Daft is head of Coca-Cola, David Johnson built an impressive reputation in his years as chairman of Campbells Soup before he retired in 1999 and Philip Bowman is CEO of British based liquor giant Allied Domecq. Ultimately though, impressive as these others are, none has the credentials to replace any of the chosen six. James Wolfensohn, president of the World Bank, could certainly have made a contribution. He was in fact approached, but at the time he had just completed a visit to Australia where he had spoken several times on issues similar to those raised here. He was concerned about overplaying the role of gratuitous adviser and declined on that account.

It should also be acknowledged that there are important and informed business figures resident in Australia. There are Australian-based companies now making a mark on the world whose CEOs might easily have been considered. One thinks of Frank Lowy's Westfield group, of transport and logistics group Brambles, of construction company Lend Lease, of Qantas or of

Foster's with its international wine and brewing interests. They are impressive, but none commands the international respect of the six chosen here. Companies such as Philip Morris, Ford and News Corporation are not just multinationals, they are giants. British Airways and Rio Tinto do not rank far behind them.

In the end, the six individuals whose views are represented in this book are uniquely qualified. Each of the companies they represent is not only a significant global player, but represents an area of key importance to Australia. Leigh Clifford's Rio Tinto is a giant in mineral resource development, still Australia's biggest export earner. Geoff Bible's Philip Morris, through Kraft, is a major player in food processing in Australia and the company bases a significant international IT operation here also. Rod Eddington is hugely informed on tourism — widely tipped as our best export growth prospect — and his company owns a major shareholding in Qantas. Jac Nasser has intimate knowledge of manufacturing, particularly motor vehicle manufacture which has become the surprise packet of our export performance with sales now above A$4 billion a year. Add Lord May's expertise in science and in tertiary education (another export growth area) and you have a good cross-section of the industries on which Australia's future seems destined to depend.

When this project was first conceived a decision was made not to furnish the participants with a list of specific questions because this would have shaped or distorted their perspectives. They would have been talking to the author's agenda, not their own.

For example, had they been specifically asked to comment on the competitiveness of our industrial relations system and our levels of taxation there is no doubt that they would have done so — and done it thoughtfully. But the appearance of regular comments from each of them on these issues throughout the book might have given the impression that these were issues they universally considered critical. Unprompted, these issues did not rank highly among the interviewee's concerns. Often, what people don't say is as revealing as what they do.

For that reason each of the six was asked in advance only to give their views on the outlook for Australia, the various forces which would shape that future and, if they wished, some thoughts on strategies that Australia might want to adopt in order to address future challenges. Within that broad framework they were invited to canvass any issues they thought relevant.

What is surprising is that this very broad and open-ended framework produced a significant degree of consensus. While each approached discussion initially from various perspectives — some beginning with a historical sweep, others with an analysis of strengths and opportunities — all spent some time on common themes such as migration, education, globalism and the social frameworks that give Australia a comparative advantage over many other mid-size nations.

This degree of consensus is both instructive and reassuring. There is sufficient diversity in the participants' proposals to suggest they are the fruits of individual input rather than any collective business viewpoint, but sufficient consistency in the areas of discussion to allow Australians to draw some overall conclusions. Six conflicting or unrelated viewpoints would not have been particularly illuminating.

Notwithstanding the impressive specialist knowledge which each of the participants has in his own field, it may be a mistake to think of these people as technical experts only. Their interests are broader than that.

One of the inspirations for the project was my experience as a public affairs consultant, a job which gave me the opportunity to spend time with some of Australia's resident business leaders — discussing issues, drafting speeches and observing work practices. What was fascinating was not the leaders' predictable views on company performance, but the occasional more personal diversions into broader social issues. Often their views were insightful and their philosophical positions unexpected.

Almost by tradition in Australia, business figures speak publicly only on issues that affect their own company. Those who break this tradition tend to be criticised for dragging their companies into divisive social debates that offer no benefit to shareholders. In consequence we have a situation where some of the nation's keenest analytical brains speak publicly only to represent their direct commercial interests. The public and the media in consequence have come to regard business leaders as merely the voice of sectional interests.

This book is something of an attempt to break that mould. It was thus rewarding that — unsolicited — the business figures departed at times from the traditional sectional concerns of taxation, industrial relations, wage rates and economic management and cast their gaze to broader concepts like immigration and multiculturalism, education and science, political transparency, social cohesion and the role of philanthropy.

Perhaps that is not surprising. Increasingly the major shareholders in large public companies are not wealthy private investors but superannuation funds representing the retirement hopes of millions of ordinary Australians. The once stark divisions between the interests of labour and the interests of capital have become just a fraction more blurred. Even the traditional gulf between town and gown — between business and academia — is being bridged: universities are no longer ivory towers but incubators of the knowledge that is increasingly the basis of modern wealth, while corporations are the workplaces to which most of the ever rising number of university graduates will eventually turn.

No doubt at other times and in other places the business leaders will need to revert to voicing their more traditional sectional concerns. But for this project at least, they abandoned their traditional masks and talked openly and at times passionately about the future of Australia and the directions it might take. They offered their unique knowledge and insights as informed citizens, as parents and as grandparents. As Australians.

CHAPTER ONE

A nation in transition

A generation ago this book would not have been either possible or necessary.

Not possible because there would have been few Australians in command of major global organisations. Not necessary because Australia's international competitiveness was then less relevant. It would have been pointless to ask whether Australian workers could compete on equal terms with producers in Asia or the US; we never expected them to. We had tariffs to balance that equation.

All that has changed. Paul Kelly, journalist, political commentator and historian, titled his superb history of Australia during the eighties and nineties *The End of Certainty*. The title aptly reflects his central thesis that over the last two decades of the twentieth century Australia progressively abandoned the philosophies and institutions which it had earlier adopted to protect it from the outside world.

This was not so much a choice as something forced on Australians by both the inherent shortcomings of their own system and the rapid changes occurring outside their borders. Nonetheless, it meant Australia entered the twenty-first century pursuing — perhaps a trifle reluctantly and certainly nervously — a course unlike any in its history. It developed into an outward-looking trading nation with a multi-regional focus abroad and a cosmopolitan population at home operating in an increasingly deregulated workplace and marketplace.

For the first time in almost a century, Australians are willing to stake their prosperity on their productivity.

To understand what a fundamental shift that represents, it is worth returning again to Kelly and what he calls The Australian Settlement that underpinned our previous philosophies.

Australia was probably the first nation in the world to decree that wage levels and working conditions should be fixed by social need rather than by productivity and economic forces. In 1907 Henry Higgins, president of the newly founded Federal Court of Conciliation and Arbitration, established in the Harvester Judgment a minimum pay rate calculated at what he believed a man needed to support a family of five in acceptable circumstances. The concept was rapidly extended (with higher awards for more skilled workers) to give Australia's largely unionised workers a centrally administered wage schedule that covered all industries.

It was possible at that time to fix wage rates independently of productivity because Australia also embraced a broad-ranging system of tariff protection. If Australian companies paying these wages could not compete with imported products, then duties were levied on foreign-made goods to ensure the balance was restored. This of course made it difficult for Australian manufacturers to export, but that was less of a problem in an age when the overwhelming bulk of exports were primary products; when Australia had a quasi-monopoly on fine wool and when a good proportion of other farm-based exports went to Britain which offered 'Empire preference' (later to become Commonwealth preference). To further ensure the support and survival of primary producers, various marketing and regulatory authorities were set up to shield them (to a degree at least) from the vagaries of international commodity prices.

(In 1907, the year of Higgins' decision, wool supplied about half of Australia's total commodity exports of 60 million pounds with wheat and flour supplying another 6 million pounds. Almost half of all our exports went to Britain and much of the rest went to other British Empire countries.)

Underpinning all this was the White Australia Policy. The ostensible reason for the policy was to prevent an influx of poor Asian workers willing to live, in the jargon of the day, 'off the smell of an oily rag' and so undercut Australian pay rates and working conditions. Equally fundamental was a strong element of racism; Australia was to remain an essentially British, or at the very least European, society.

It could be said that Australia's was an economy built around a lifestyle — and that lifestyle placed a high-value on evening and weekend leisure. (It is often claimed that the Australian passion for sport can be traced to the fact that we were the first nation to give workers a five and a half day week. In an era when stricter religious observance discouraged the playing of spectator sports on Sundays, Australians with their work-free Saturday afternoons had a unique opportunity.)

Although these foundations were laid in the first decade after Federation, they endured and were perhaps even reinforced by the philosophies of protectionism and nationalism that developed as a result of the Great Depression and the Second World War. They were still substantially in place into the 1970s and even beyond.

Any Australian over 50 who looks back now on the Australia of their youth is stunned to realise what an extraordinarily regulated society it was. The author remembers that in Perth in the late 1960s new liquor licences would not be granted if they were likely to provide competition for an existing hotel. Shopping hours were heavily regulated; department stores were five and a half day a week operations with no late-night shopping permitted. Milk bars (what are now convenience stores) could stay open outside these hours but the range of goods they were allowed to sell was limited and rigidly policed. And woe betide any entrepreneurial soul in Victoria who offered to sell hardware to do-it-yourself handymen on Sundays. That was strictly illegal (and prompted the famous quote from a talkback radio host that with the licensing of brothels, it was now legal to buy a screw on Sunday, but not a nail). The workforce was heavily unionised and the unions, backed by the courts, defined which tasks could be carried out by members of which unions.

This cosy, insulated world eventually proved unsustainable. One of the first elements to crack was the White Australia Policy, abandoned in name in 1966 (in response to a growing international stigma attached to race-based policies) and in practice over the succeeding fifteen to twenty years (due to the growing economic power of Asia and its importance as a trading partner).

Trade patterns also changed. Wool, which in its peak year of 1950–51 provided about 66 per cent of Australia's exports came under challenge from synthetic fibres and by 1977–78 was providing just under 10 per cent. Compounding this, Britain in 1973 joined the European Common Market, forcing Australian meat and dairy products to compete with Europe's highly subsidised producers. The primary industry export base on which our economy had rested was collapsing.

In purely monetary terms the collapse of these traditional markets was offset by the spectacular growth in minerals exports, particularly to a resurgent Asia. Coal, iron and alumina replaced wool and wheat as our major exports — but the change had more significance than merely propping up a fragile balance of payments account.

Where we had enjoyed a dominant position in the supply of fine wool — an edge in both quality and efficiency — we enjoyed no such luxury with energy and minerals. They are commodities in which price and reliability of supply are critical factors and the productive efficiency of our workforce thus became a crucial economic factor.

A side effect of this was that Asia became our major trading partner, forcing a severe rethink of traditional attitudes.

In the last decades of the twentieth century the very nature of wealth creation changed. Services began to overtake goods as the major component of post-industrial economies. Technology created valuable new products which meant a company like Microsoft could create multi-billion dollar wealth from developing computer codes. Others could make fortunes from pharmaceuticals or even electronic games. Primary products still had a place in the world economy, but they were not the growth areas. Where did that leave Australia with its inefficient manufacturing sector and its high dependence on primary products for export earnings?

In Asia, first Japan, then Hong Kong, Singapore, Korea, Taiwan and China enjoyed dramatic economic growth. While that created huge new markets for Australian materials — indeed they became our biggest export markets — it also put pressure on Australian manufacturers, for these countries were aggressive exporters. To shut out their manufactured goods was to put at risk the exports on which our economy depended.

At the same time, economic philosophies throughout the world changed. The protectionist policies which many countries had followed since the 1920s were progressively abandoned (at least for manufactures) following the success of the European Common Market and its eventual successor the European Union. Every country suddenly wanted to be part of a trade bloc. If you wanted to export your own goods, you needed to open your door to others. All the evidence seemed to show that closed economies prospered less than open ones.

It is doubtful that the majority of Australians understood the totality of all these changes and the impact on them, but they became aware that the old system was not serving them as well as it once did. In the late nineteenth century Australians were widely regarded as having probably the highest living standards in the world. A century later they could visit Tokyo and be aware that they could not afford to go to places frequented by middle-class Japanese; where once they had visited London and felt affluent among the locals, they now felt more like poor relations; they learnt that Singaporeans had overtaken them in the wealth stakes. (By 2000 Singapore had a per capita GDP of US$22 966 compared to Australia's $19 883. Britain was ahead of both at US23 815 while for the USA the figure was a whopping $36 149).

Australian governments could not ignore these realities. Successively the Hawke, Keating and Howard governments set about dismantling what remained of the Australian Settlement in an effort to make the country more competitive: tariffs were progressively reduced, or even removed, and the restrictions on foreign capital investment were eased. The old central wage-fixing system was progressively modified to allow more flexible enterprise agreements; amalgamations reduced the number of unions (and with it the number of demarcation disputes). The dollar was floated to allow its value to more accurately reflect our production costs and our trading position. Australian governments sought to engage more with Asia and to become meaningful participants in regional trade groupings and Australia sought to become a member of the North American Free Trade Agreement while maintaining its Asian links. National and State monopolies in energy, transport and communications were broken up, commercialised or privatised. Efforts were made to introduce more open competition everywhere in the economy.

These changes were not painless. To become competitive some businesses (including former government-owned utilities) shed staff. Denied tariff protection, some companies moved manufacturing operations offshore to countries with lower labour costs; others were forced out of business; some survived by paring staff and increasing productivity. Less restrictive foreign investment criteria saw a succession of Australian companies taken over by multinationals, causing some Australians to anguish over a perceived loss of sovereignty. Unions, despite their support for many of the reforms, felt their power and influence diminish (and on the docks and in the construction industry led fierce resistance). By 2002 there were more people self-employed or working as contractors in Australia than there were union members.

Almost everyone felt the new business environment to be harsher and more stressful. 'No gain without pain' might be the slogan plastered on the walls of a thousand sports clubs, but the message felt distinctly less heroic when applied to economic change where pain came in the form of unemployment or job insecurity.

Yet the changes also brought some striking successes. From the mid-1990s Australia enjoyed a period of strong economic growth — a growth rate which outstripped other developed nations. Trade did diversify. By 2002 Australia could list 24 countries which each took more than $A1 billion of exports and 60 countries which took more than A$100 million. Against everything they had believed for the best part of a century, Australians found they could — at least in some industries — manufacture and sell sophisticated goods in competition with both developed countries and low-wage developing nations. Exports of these products (statistically recorded as Extensively Transformed Manufactures) climbed 41 per cent in the five years to June 2001. Growth in tourism and education further improved the picture.

It took time for these gains to become apparent, however, and there is no doubt that many Australians clung for a long time — and some still do — to the hope that we could somehow maintain our previous sheltered position. One of the recurring themes of Don Watson's history of Paul Keating's prime ministership *Recollections of a Bleeding Heart*, is the disappointment Keating felt that so much of the electorate refused to acknowledge the scale of his achievements in bringing about these changes, both as prime minister and as treasurer to previous prime minister Bob Hawke. There was insufficient recognition, he felt, of both the necessity to reshape Australia to meet its new environment, the scale of change that had been accomplished and the rewards those changes would bring — and indeed were bringing, even as he was voted from office. He cannot claim, however, that the public voted for a return to the old order for the Howard government introduced a raft of further changes to taxation, industrial relations and welfare.

Future historians will no doubt debate at length the credit and blame that various political leaders can share for the changes that have taken place in Australia in recent decades. They will do so armed with the detailed knowledge of how well Australia completed its transformation and the level of prosperity that transformation achieved.

Current Australians are denied the luxury of that hindsight. We need to make decisions now, at a personal, corporate and national level, about how best to deal with the world that is evolving around us.

It is in that context that we seek the views of the six international leaders here. For us this is a brave new world; for them it is an environment in which they have operated for some years. Each has personally triumphed in a competitive global market. They have not so much seen the future as visited it and succeeded in it.

CHAPTER TWO

What makes a global high-flyer?

What sort of people are these leaders of global industry? Interesting — and in some ways surprising.

We expect our corporate leaders to be shrewd negotiators and demanding administrators and we know they must have a good brain and a strong streak of determination to have got where they are. We also have to accept that in the world they inhabit it would be almost impossible not to develop a strong sense of your own importance. These things must be taken as given.

But some of their other qualities are less expected: they are all, for example, quite engaging personalities. Across a coffee table each talks with a quiet sincerity; weaving detail into a bigger, more integral picture in a way that can generate a degree of excitement.

It is not just their personalities, for each is very different. Jac Nasser, for example, exudes intellectual energy. He talks with a brisk but measured flow and ideas appear to emerge fully developed. The words are chosen with precision and there are few hesitations or clarifications. The pace of delivery suggests that the picture he is revealing is already totally clear in his mind.

Rupert Murdoch is at the other end of the scale: he's unashamedly thoughtful and doesn't mind if you watch the process. There can be long pauses while he evaluates the point he wants to make and the words with which he wants to express it.

He'll talk fluently for some minutes but at a critical juncture will pause, fingers arched almost prayer-like at his chin, while he painstakingly selects the next sentence. Like Nasser though, the words once selected are precise; he rarely needs to clarify a point.

The others are somewhere in between, with Rod Eddington perhaps a little closer to the pace of Nasser and Geoff Bible a touch closer to Murdoch, though given to more animated bursts as he warms to favourite themes. Leigh Clifford strikes a balance.

With such diverse styles, what makes them collectively such commanding communicators? It is the way they construct their presentation and the way they develop a rapport with the listener.

Each of the business leaders delivered a vision for Australia. In retrospect, it's clear that each delivered his vision in a more or less business style — either an analysis of strengths, weaknesses, opportunities, threats, and options or, alternatively, a review of the existing situation, an exposition of the impacts of likely change and the policy options which flow from that.

And yet it never felt like that at the time. It never felt formularised; there was always a feeling of freshness.

Each of them was also quietly motivating, leaving you with the feeling that if Australia can get this right, the future can be quite exciting. Yet no-one could be more removed than these men from the image of the traditional motivator: they talked quietly without theatrics; there were no extravagant gestures, no buzzwords, few acronyms, no slogans, none of the usual clichés.

This absence of clichés, more than anything, distinguishes them from the common herd of middle management. By expressing things in their own words, they give ownership to the ideas and a sense of innovation. Even where the concepts are familiar, they never sound parroted or hackneyed.

A big part of their capacity to command involvement relates to the old truism, that to be interesting, be interested. Each managed to convey a real sense of engagement with the question of Australia's future. It was signalled in the originality of the ideas and the language, in a quickening of the voice when they warmed to a particular issue and the subtle shifts in body language that signalled scepticism or excitement as various issues were canvassed. Having committed precious time to the project, they gave it their full interest and energy for that time.

It was their ability to do this in a quiet, personal way — in a way that suggested they were sincere and not just putting on a show — that marked them as genuine motivators and also as effective teachers. They could give import and depth to an issue.

Interestingly, Bob May, the academic and in that sense, professional teacher, exhibited this quality least, though perhaps for good reason. He was courteous, equally lucid in his presentation, and far more thorough than the others in documenting his points. His knowledge of the issues was copious and he was nothing short of brilliant in presenting complex issues in a manner that made them understandable to a lay listener without trivialising them.

The difference was that he presented them with a degree of detachment. He eschewed certainty; he laid the information before you and explained the various hypotheses that were drawn from it, but — perhaps as a good scientist should — he did so with calculated objectivity. Unmistakably the message was: this is the conclusion I have reached and this is the way I have reached it, but I am not selling you my conclusion, I am presenting it.

The others were not so objective. They allowed their enthusiasms to show, drew you into their vision, hinted at the prizes to be won.

I suppose this should be no surprise. A scientist is not supposed to reflect his emotional attachment to an outcome; only to present the evidence. For a modern CEO, on the other hand, the ability to convey a vision is a key quality. If they want to keep the share price up or go to the market for a capital raising they need to convince the hotshot young analysts from the institutions — the investment funds that control billions of dollars of superannuation and savings — that their chosen course for the company is the right one.

Analysts with their supercomputers can crunch columns of figures in minutes. They can tell you in seconds the difference that a few cents' variance in exchange rates can make to a company's interest payments or export receipts. But computers can't sense a vision for a company's future, or a faith that there is a clearly mapped strategy. Investors need to feel confident in the people as well as the numbers; there needs to be a belief that, whatever unexpected difficulties arise, the management will have the answers. Only a leader who has both intellect and communication skills can engender that sort of confidence. These leaders possess such qualities in abundance.

CHAPTER THREE

Jac Nasser

With hindsight, it was a silly question to ask of a cab driver in Dearborn, Michigan: Do you know the Ford headquarters?

Dearborn is Ford City, the birthplace of Henry Ford and the capital of the Ford empire. The main thoroughfares carry names like Fairlane and Mercury; most people here work at Ford and the airport exists largely to bring them from across the USA, Europe, Asia, Africa, Latin America and Australia to the steel and glass tower set in parklands that is the company's global headquarters.

Asking the driver if he knows the building is like asking a Washington cabbie if he knows the Capitol. The driver's contemptuous look says it all, but we are pushed for time and the cab is trundling along in steady traffic, so the next question is whether we can be there in time for a 10 a.m. appointment.

'Probably not,' says the cabbie, 'but you won't be too late — maybe a few minutes. Maybe five.' The tone makes it clear he doesn't rush for anyone.

'I'd rather not be late at all,' I explain, 'I'm seeing the boss.'

The cabbie is unimpressed, but then American cabbies make a point of being unimpressed.

'The big boss,' I add. 'The chief.'

'Mr Nasser?' The cab accelerates noticeably. We start overtaking and we swing into the Ford forecourt at 9.59 a.m. precisely. In this part of the world, Jac Nasser is a king.

It is a kingship that is under threat even as we arrive. Press reports say the Ford family who still own much of the company's stock are planning to dethrone the bustling Australian from the CEO's chair. He has made dramatic changes at Ford, trying to adapt an organisation founded 100 years ago to the needs of the twenty-first century, and though many analysts are impressed by his intellectual grasp of the issues, they say the rapid changes have earned him enemies — and with Ford now facing some problems, the knives are out. The TV crews hovering in the foyer, awaiting a scheduled announcement from him, are proof of the heightening speculation.

Yet on the executive floor, the man himself is waiting in his office doorway, grinning almost cheekily; chest thrust out to display a sweatshirt from his old college, the Royal Melbourne Institute of Technology.

For a fleeting moment — and to the delight of his watching staff — he strikes a model's pose to display the RMIT shirt, then laughs as he confesses it is not his normal office attire. 'I had one sent over because Ford has an annual day when everyone wears their old school or college jumper. I keep it here in the office. It seemed appropriate for today.'

He is disarmingly informal — he offers coffee and makes it himself — but even while putting you at ease he is making use of every second. While he pours the coffee he invites a Black American woman who has joined us to explain her role. She is there under an 'executive partnership' scheme in which junior and middle executives get to spend a few days with the CEO or other top executives.

Nasser digresses for just a minute to explain why this is necessary. In a huge organisation like Ford, executives traditionally climb the ladder in a specialised department (like law, human resources, finance or engineering) and while this gives them an awesome depth of knowledge in their special field, it also limits the breadth of their knowledge: they don't get to see how the whole jigsaw fits together. Hence, the partnership program which allows junior executives to spend time with the most senior executives and get a glimpse of the full range of issues. That means no secrets — the younger executives sit in on everything, even a discussion on Australia's future.

Jac Nasser has prepared a series of one-line reminders of items he wants to cover and he speaks to each concisely and coherently. The lucidity is impressive.

Indeed, it is almost impossible not to be impressed by Jac Nasser: he has intelligence, energy and — notwithstanding the toughness that earned him the nickname Jac the Knife — he is very personable and even charming when the occasion permits.

Jacques Nasser was born in 1947 in Amyoun, Lebanon, a mountain village north of Beirut, but his family moved to Australia in the early 1950s. After graduating from the Royal Melbourne

Institute of Technology (RMIT) in business, he joined Ford Australia as a financial analyst.

His 35-year career with Ford took him through a variety of ever more senior positions in Europe, Australia, the Philippines, Thailand, Japan, South Africa, Venezuela, Mexico, Brazil, and Argentina. He is fluent in English, Arabic, Spanish and Portuguese.

In his career with Ford he has faced almost every business environment: a military junta in Argentina, a financial meltdown in Asia, hyperinflation, closed markets, open markets, global automotive consolidation. Small wonder he now has an almost crystal vision of the way the world is evolving, politically and economically.

His input to technology and education issues and his contributions to humanitarian causes have earned him an Order of Australia, an Order of the Cedar from Lebanon and an honorary doctorate from his alma mater, RMIT.

He became CEO of the Ford Motor Company and a member of its board shortly before his fifty-first birthday.

As he climbed into the topmost ranks of Ford he sought to reshape the company for the twenty-first century, focusing on global competitiveness, closer connections to the consumer, brand/product development, increased diversity, and leadership development. He oversaw the growth and acquisition of Jaguar, Aston Martin, Volvo, Land Rover and Hertz. In addition, he restructured the Ford Motor Company. He closed plants in the US, Europe, and elsewhere and discontinued models that did not generate adequate profitability. He closed or sold unprofitable operations. He was responsible for the formation of the Premier Automotive Group and relocated Lincoln-Mercury to its new headquarters in California. He added strength to Ford's light truck and sport utility vehicles and oversaw a product revolution with the introduction of the Ford Ka and the Ford Focus as well as the sporty, two-seater Thunderbird.

It is easy with hindsight to see the difficulties of dragging a company along at such a pace. Nasser did not come from the US and had worked in every continent on the globe during his rise. He saw globalisation at its grass roots level; he saw a world in which the internet was opening up the potential to talk directly to customers rather than communicating only through dealers. He saw that the highly successful business model Ford had created over the last century needed adaptation if it was to remain globally competitive in the next.

Jac Nasser is clearly aware of the stresses such rapid change creates. Talking of Australia and those who want to abandon traditional industries in the rush to create new high-tech products, he says, 'It is a mistake we all make to think we can jump from one to the other immediately.' You suspect that is as much a personal reflection as a national one.

Nonetheless, his global experience and his efforts to map a new vision for Ford clearly overlap with his thoughts for Australia. Here his vision is equally broad. Not just economics is canvassed but wider issues like social cohesion ('My father left Lebanon because the country was being torn apart'); harmonious acceptance of immigrants (' Australia has probably done this better than anyone else') and tolerance ('We need to beware we don't become intolerant, of people with dissenting views').

He moves systematically through the spectrum, only rarely referring to his notes and occasionally asking his younger colleague for her input on contemporary issues like the US education system. His economy of words is illustrated by a discussion on education and the concerns that early specialisation can lock students into a particular career path prematurely. 'Not everyone knows where they are going — you need exit ramps,' he says succinctly.

The interview concludes, there are a few moments of sociability and we head for the door. A glance at the watch: bang on schedule.

He is already shedding the RMIT sweatshirt, but not his Australian identity. Outside his office I joke to his staff that I am in awe of him . . ., 'not because he runs Ford but because he's got a bar in Melbourne named after him.'

He overhears and his head appears round the door, beaming. 'Hey, Jac's Bar — you know it?'

Downstairs in the foyer the TV cameras and radio mikes are massing for his announcement. Soon afterwards the corporate Jacques Nasser appears, dark suit, grim face, to announce the measures he is taking to cut costs, including cutting his own executive bonus by millions of dollars. There is again, a sense of focused energy and precise thought. Even sections of the hard-nosed financial press, there to write his professional obituary, are impressed.

It is not enough to save him. A few weeks later company chairman William Clay Ford announces that Mr Nasser, the man who only eighteen months earlier had guided Ford to the greatest profit in its history, is to step down.

Jac Nasser says he is heading back to Australia to do a bit of surfing. Nobody doubts he will re-emerge in public life. The wild seas might slake that physical energy, but not the intellectual energy: that will need to find an outlet.

Why world trends are heading Australia's way

To talk of Australia in an isolated sense is to miss the point: you need to see it in the context of world trends.

If I were to look at those trends — economic, political and industrial — over the past 100 years, I'd say there have been four distinct phases, each of which effectively created the pre-conditions for its successor.

If you look at the first years of the twentieth century it was a period of intense colonisation. There was colonisation of political systems, of religion, of trade and even industrial and business systems.

Industrially, Henry Ford created an economic model for mass manufacture in the US, took that model and colonised it into Britain, Ireland, France and even Australia.

It happened very quickly, Ford was founded in the US in 1903 and was transplanted to most of the countries I mention within ten to fifteen years. When you think of the transport and communications requirements and the technology that existed at the time, it was extraordinary. I am sure that when a company — or even a country — was set up, there was a local governor type figure who, because of the communications at the time, had to exercise a lot of authority. The technology didn't permit regular discussion with head office.

That was a unique period; you can almost put a boundary around it.

Some time after World War I — though I hate to put history around wars — there was a reaction against this colonialism and an intense political nationalism developed. Some good things came of that — national pride — but also some bad, most visibly, and ultimately disastrously, in Germany, Italy and Japan.

This nationalism was economic as well as political and cultural. There was a desire to have a national view of things, a national presence in key areas. In the motor industry in Australia for example, Ford became Ford Australia and GM became General Motors-Holden's; each needed to be given a distinctive Australian identity. In the mood of the times we had to have our *own* motor industry.

In this climate of political and economic nationalism every nation felt obliged to develop its own key industries — particularly strategic industries like iron and steel, shipbuilding and advanced manufacturing. Each sought to protect and nurture these industries within its own borders through tariff barriers or other forms of assistance.

The effect was to fragment Europe, in particular, into a series of limited national markets each held in hegemony by a protected, even subsidised, local producer.

The US was not immune to these forces of protectionism and nationalism, but if it was a protected market, it was still a very large market of several hundred million people. US producers fought over a market the size of all Western Europe. There was still scope for massive economies of scale and room for competition. The world's biggest and most competitive producers were increasingly American and it was they who set the benchmarks for global trade and who had the resources for global expansion. European producers, built around their smaller and regulated national markets, found it hard to compete. Intense European nationalism had, ironically, created the conditions for dominance by US multinationals.

By the mid-1950s a resurgent Western Europe realised its problem. Beginning with the coal and steel industries, West European nations progressively moved to create a single regional market, free of internal restrictions, to give European companies the same opportunities as their US counterparts. Economic cooperation was accompanied by political cooperation and the European Community evolved into the European Union. The age of regionalism was born, even if protectionism lingered (and still lingers) in many countries in politically sensitive sectors such as agriculture.

I can vividly remember how aghast and shocked Australians were when they learnt that Britain would no longer favour Australian butter and cheese. We were witnessing a major transition — from colonial-national eras to regionalism and we needed to adjust our thinking very quickly to these new realities.

The success of Europe's free trade experiment and the prosperity its members enjoyed, led other nations to look down the same path and the European Union was soon followed by the Association of South-East Asian Nations, the North American Free Trade Agreement and the Andes Pact. Any country not in a regional grouping sought to forge an alliance with one through associate membership or some other special relationship.

That period lasted from the sixties into the nineties. Elements of it persist today, but we are shifting into what is often called — though I hate the term — globalisation; globalisation of almost everything.

This is being driven not by wars and ideology — though we have seen the collapse of communist states — but by technology and by the elimination of many trade barriers. It is also driven by an unbelievable transparency in communications. You can give some credit for the fall of communist states to the fact that people were able to see what was happening elsewhere and compare living standards and the technology that was available. You didn't need to be very insightful to see the difference between the Trabant produced in the Eastern bloc and the cars we in the West were producing.

What has emerged is that trade relations in this global era are in some ways a logical extension of regionalism. If the trade opportunities within regional groupings were stimulating, the opportunities for trade between these massive (and increasingly prosperous) markets were even more attractive.

And if those inside these trading blocs of largely developed nations wanted access to markets beyond, there was equal pressure the other way. Even the poorest developing countries wanted access to affluent markets like the US for the low-cost consumer goods they could produce. Hence the pressure for wider trade liberalisation that has dominated the past decade, boosted by a desire to access the new technologies — and sometimes capital markets too.

Where does Australia fit into all this?

Interestingly, Australia participated in each phase — though some more than others. If Australia were a company, I would characterise it as a nimble, very agile, diverse company that probably doesn't have one single strength, but is a great all-rounder with capacities in a range of areas: an organisation with a tremendous capacity for transformation. This capacity for change is in the culture now and I see it as one of Australia's biggest strengths.

I don't want to harp on this, but if you look back to the abandonment of the White Australia Policy — the policy which endured for a while, even when officially it wasn't a policy — there are very few countries that could make that type of transformation as quickly, as well and as peacefully as Australia. I can't think of any other country, not even the US, as good as it is at assimilating new cultures and new ideas. I think Australia is remarkable.

We are a small island, in population terms at least, and a small market. You can look at that as a weakness — and it is — but it was more of a weakness in the past periods I have described than it is in the era we are entering.

So, I see the trends heading very much in Australia's direction.

With any transformation you can't make the entire leap immediately, even though trying to do that is a mistake we all make. We don't want to lose Australia's existing strengths — our efficient agriculture and mining, our creativity and innovation and the ability to do things in a very low-cost, efficient manner. We don't want to lose these things as we develop new strengths like tourism, e-commerce and education — things we can build using one of the most diverse populations anywhere in the world.

I'm not sure everyone in Australia realises what an asset we have in that diverse population. When I went back to run Ford Australia after having worked overseas, one of the things I was told was that it was going to be hard to run the Australian plants efficiently because the workforce spoke seventeen languages. That's a problem? I thought it was a plus! I thought that if you were a global business leader and somebody handed you a group of energetic, courageous people, who between them spoke seventeen languages, you'd say: 'That's an asset. How do we do something with that?'

There are certain things that Australia does very well.

Traditionally we've been good at mining and agriculture, but there are new areas where Australia can have a competitive advantage: the whole area of design creativity, of e-commerce and internet technology and of taking ideas and putting those ideas into the marketplace.

Whether you look at medicine or power steering pumps you find there are Australians with this capacity to take ideas and develop them. I don't know what it is — part of it is the education system, part of it is just the way you grow up in Australia — but there is something, some characteristic that gives many Australians an edge. You see it in the over-representation of Australians in key positions in international organisations.

I believe the smallness of many Australian enterprises actually makes them good incubators of leadership and business skills. You get a broader view of the whole enterprise at a much earlier stage of your career. This is an unbelievable advantage. Smaller companies don't allow the luxury of specialisation in a narrow field. You need to be a bit of a jack of all trades — literate in just about all areas of the business and specialist in something. That's a bit of a template for leadership.

In Australia I was managing small companies in my twenties. That wouldn't happen so much in the US; you'd more likely be working your way up through some specialised area — the legal department, finance or whatever, developing a very deep understanding of your own field, but somewhat isolated from other departments. It is just a different career path.

Nonetheless, I believe that having broader involvement at an early stage of your career can be helpful in giving you a full picture of how the organisation fits together. I think that is not true just of business; I suspect it applies in other areas as well in Australia, like education and the cultural fields.

It is something we don't want to lose. As long as we have that we have a vibrant, robust economy.

This brings me to a different point, one which perhaps reflects my background. My parents left Lebanon because the country was disintegrating. You can't have a vibrant healthy country if you don't have vibrant enterprises; but on the other hand you can't have the reverse either. They go together. You can't say I don't want this industry or I don't like that one; that's the start of real deterioration. Strong communities, strong companies, strong enterprises, sound values — they all go together.

Part of that strength is harmony: a spirit of inclusion. It is the government and the educational system, the health system, the unions and enterprises all working together.

I get dismayed when I see open conflict. I guess some conflict is inevitable, but it degrades the long-term quality of society if you don't get people working together. There's got to be a place for everyone in the system — not 'I'll include you, but I don't like your views, so not you.'

But to return to my point about world trends heading in Australia's direction, I see these flexible Australian companies finding niche opportunities in this global marketplace — opportunities that multinational giants aren't flexible enough and quick-reacting enough to seize ... or opportunities that perhaps aren't big enough to attract the attention of the huge companies but which can be very attractive to smaller companies.

I see Australians with their adaptability and their ability to take ideas and develop them finding opportunities in this very open commercial world.

Perhaps even the smallness of our capital markets is less a disadvantage in this new era than it was previously. The heavy industries and mass manufacturing that were the cornerstone of economic power in past eras needed massive capital to start up and to be competitive on a world scale. There are new technology-based opportunities emerging which have different capital requirements: not only are these requirements sometimes smaller, but in a world of freer capital markets, if you have the ideas and the know-how, you will attract capital — whether that be from within or beyond Australia.

All this creates opportunities — and we have a democratic, law-based society with an educated workforce that holds some attractions for investors if the opportunities are there. For those reasons we have some grounds for optimism about Australia's place in this new phase of world development.

You mentioned education. How do you rate Australia's education system?

I've got four kids and two of the girls went through the Australian system — Melbourne University — and one has lived in several countries and been largely educated in Britain and the US.

Using that experience as a yardstick, I'd say one concern about the Australian system is that it tends to force you to specialise too early. Some people are into their twenties before they really know what they want to do. Not everyone knows where they are going — you need exit ramps.

The US system is more generalist, but on the other hand it is almost mandatory in the US to do a postgraduate degree; I think it is still less so in Australia. Both systems have their points, but I would prefer a more generalist approach.

Also, in the US tertiary education is considered almost a right and I kind of like that. I think in Australia there's still a feeling that if you are not bright enough or focused enough, you miss out.

But while I do like the idea that everyone should have access to tertiary education, I'm also a strong supporter of the apprenticeship system — which you can look at as a mentoring system, devised before the term became fashionable.

In Australia we still do apprenticeships pretty well. So does Germany and there are some really top people at Ford who have come up through the German apprenticeship system and then gone on to later do tertiary studies. One, now a very senior executive, went on to do a doctorate, which gives him a terrific background — grounded in both the practicalities of production and a very deep knowledge of theory.

Is the relationship between business and the education sector different in the US compared to Australia?

In the US, if you look at community involvement — at involvement with society in general — then corporations are deeply involved. Not just with charitable donations, but actively involved with communities around their plants — not just with cash but through employees contributing to environmental events and cultural events. And with universities: university research is heavily funded by and supported by corporations.

The investment of corporations in university recruitment is also unbelievable. The resources allocated to it — not just with the students themselves but with the universities direct; fostering a two-way understanding of both what the corporations are looking for from the education sector and conversely what the universities are trying to achieve.

The corporate relationship with the community in the US is not perfect, nowhere near perfect, but it is the best I have seen. When I first came to the US, I was surprised — you could almost say shocked — at how much involvement a company like Ford has with the community, versus what would be expected of a company in Australia.

And I'd say Australia is ahead of Europe. In Europe people would look at it and say: 'That's not a corporate responsibility; the government will look after that,' whether it is funding research or making a charitable donation. There doesn't seem to be a history there of giving in the broader social sense. In the US there is.

You talked of Australia being attractive for investment: is our tax system competitive?

I think so. A tax system doesn't have to be competitive in every detail at every point as long as overall it is competitive. It is important too that the underlying principles are clear. In general I think the Australian Tax Office has come a long way over the years in its administration.

But the tax system is just one element in the investment decision. It is important, but only as part of an overall mix. There are other things like stability, an educated workforce and the rule of law which also weigh significantly.

All in all, Australia has many of these fundamentals in place. If Australians can grasp the opportunities that technology and the emerging world trends present, I think the future can be good.

CHAPTER FOUR

Robert May

The environment in which you find Lord May of Oxford AC, Kt is so thoroughly British that it comes as a pleasant surprise that he introduces himself as Bob.

He is a professor at Oxford but is also President of the Royal Society, the oldest and probably most famous scientific society in the world, and it is in the society's offices in St James, London, that he offers to meet. It is a building that is steeped in history, with a wide forecourt designed for a time when dignitaries arrived by horse and carriage (it was once the German Embassy but confiscated in World War I and presented to the Royal Society) and a foyer that houses a gold mace presented to the society in 1660 by King Charles II.

The walls are hung with heavy-framed portraits of past presidents — many of them the great names of British science — and as you walk these hallways you begin to grasp what an extraordinary accolade it has been for Bob May, an Australian who came to Britain via the US, to have been elected by his peers to that post.

Yet a glance at his CV reveals that this is merely one of a host of accolades. The Australian public largely knows him as the man who was selected by British Prime Minister Tony Blair to be Britain's chief scientific adviser (and in that role helped develop a blueprint to ensure Britain remains a major technological power), but since graduating from the University of Sydney he has been awarded some of the world's most coveted science prizes and been honoured by governments and institutions around the globe. The surprise is not that he was elected to President of the Royal Society but that he is not a household name in Australia.

Initially enrolled in Chemical Engineering at the University of Sydney, Robert May completed a BSc and a PhD in Theoretical Physics. He spent two years lecturing at Harvard University, then returned to Sydney where, aged just 33, he became Professor of Theoretical Physics.

In the early seventies he began to shift his focus to the study of first animal and later plant communities. He moved to Princeton University in the US as Professor of Zoology in 1973 and subsequently became Chairman of the university research board with broad administrative responsibility for all research. In 1988 he moved to Britain and Oxford University as a Royal Society research professor and he now holds a professorship jointly in the Department of Zoology, Oxford University, and at Imperial College, London.

His research has focused on how plant and animal populations are structured and how they respond to change and to threats (including disease and viruses) and the rates and causes of extinction.

He has been awarded the US$500 000 (A$900 000) Royal Swedish Academy's Crafoord Prize (ecology's equivalent of a Nobel Prize); the SF500 000 (A$625 000) Swiss-Italian Balzan Prize (presented by the President of Italy for 'seminal contributions to understanding biodiversity'); and the ¥50 million (A$760 000) Japanese Blue Planet Prize (for developing fundamental tools for ecological conservation planning).

His books and contributions to scientific publications run to hundreds and he has been awarded honorary degrees from half a dozen universities around the world.

Notwithstanding all this, he is initially hesitant about offering opinions on Australia, because of the time he has spent away. When he is persuaded that his work in developing a program to advance British science and science-based industries gives him insights which even the industrial leaders cannot share, he relents but insists that he can only talk on these issues — 'within his field.'

He is a trim figure (he lists his hobbies as hiking and tennis) and his manner is slightly formal but courteous. He apologises in advance that he will have to interrupt the planned schedule to take one important phone call (which turns out to be from Britain's Science Minister, Lord Sainsbury).

The formality is reinforced by the tendency, noted earlier, to present his material in a detached manner. He supports his assertions by providing copies of scientific papers, and is transparent about the deductive processes that lead to his conclusions. On the occasions when we stray into less quantifiable areas, like social attitudes, he is meticulous in prefacing his remarks with, 'It is my observation that . . .'

His memory is excellent and he quotes statistics easily, but when he does so he makes a short note to send you copies of the material — which are duly supplied. His presentation is masterful for his ability to present the complexities of issues without losing the thread of the central argument and to simplify without sounding patronising.

He's so good at communicating complex issues that you think he should be hosting a TV science series — and his CV reveals that in fact he was a consultant to David Attenborough's epic nature series *State of the Planet*.

But the difficulties of turning scientist into presenter are obvious: Robert May's knowledge is incomparable, but it is not easy to imagine him casting off his scientific detachment and delivering his views with the sort of whispered excitement that is Attenborough's trademark.

Which probably explains why Attenborough is an acclaimed TV presenter, but Robert May is possibly the world's most acclaimed scientist. It is also why Lord May's views are so valuable to this project: they are based on a level of detailed research and objectivity which few people in Australia could hope to replicate.

Creating a successful science base

I must begin with a qualification: I left Australia in 1972 and spent sixteen years at Princeton in the US and then fourteen years here in Britain and although I've been back to Australia almost every year since 1980, I don't feel familiar enough with what is happening there to comment on that. I'm more familiar with what is happening this side of the world.

But, you have spent some time addressing how a nation might adapt to a world in which knowledge is the new currency; as to how a country can make that transition.

Yes, but let me first go back a step further and say something that is less frequently said but which puts one parameter on these discussions. If you go back 100 years, in most countries about 50 per cent of the workforce was on the land — in Britain it was about 35 per cent, because Britain was ahead in that particular revolution. The energy subsidies of daily life were much less and in general it took the efforts of about half the population just to produce the necessities of life. Today you can produce the necessities with what? — 20 per cent of the labour force, maybe a bit more, maybe a bit less — but whatever, the economy is in a structural sense totally different.

I'm giving a talk at the Natural History Museum tonight on the environmental crisis and some of the obvious points are that we should halt population growth, recycle more and be more conservation minded. But that leaves the question: If we consume less, what will create employment?

These questions also underlie the debate on how developed countries can build their knowledge-based economy to create and produce the sort of widgets that people want to buy — and do it before the market becomes flooded with them.

Look at some of the events that have occurred in recent times because people have overestimated these markets. Look at some of the telecommunications companies and what has happened when they have grossly overestimated the number of widgets [gadgets] or services they can sell. How big is the market for new wants and needs? Is it infinite? Can we go on creating new demand that will maintain high levels of employment?

I don't feel entirely comfortable talking about developing new economic bases without a deeper understanding of these questions. But that doesn't make me different from anybody else. So, for the purposes of this discussion we need to assume that all economic goods are just symbols in a set of equations that economists get Nobel Prizes for. We are asking merely how we expand our science base to provide greater benefits within this current economic model.

Within that framework, the question is how do we develop an innovative and commercially successful science base — and those two things are not necessarily identical, as I shall explain shortly.

Funding levels for science are obviously one important element, but they are not the only one. It is a more complex process than that.

Indeed, I sometimes liken those who see the development of science as only a function of money to those New Guinea cargo cultists who saw aeroplanes disgorging cargo at airports and immediately started clearing land around their own village so that the planes would come to them too. They were right in thinking that the planes couldn't come unless there was a flat area to land on, but they didn't understand that a cleared space was not in itself the solution; you needed to do a lot more to get aircraft to start arriving with loads of goodies.

In the same vein, while adequate funding is hugely important for the development of science and science based industries, cash alone is no guarantee that the rewards, both scientific and commercial, will follow. There are other factors which must be addressed simultaneously: these include how and where the money is spent and how research is structured and directed. Even things like national attitudes to entrepreneurial risk-taking can play a part.

For example, some countries achieve more for their expenditure on science than others. Paradoxically, countries with highly focused, centrally directed research programs appear to be less productive than those which allow individual researchers more freedom to follow their own interests. On the whole, universities appear to produce more advances per dollar spent on science than do dedicated research institutes.

How do you measure scientific performance? One index is to measure the number of peer-reviewed scientific papers published by scientists from various countries in scientific journals and to quantify that in relation to population size. You can also check the number of times papers from various countries are cited as references by other scientists, or cited as inspiration in patent applications. There is now a huge database available on this; something like 10 million papers published over ten years and 100 million references.

These provide some interesting comparisons.

Take France and Germany. Both are advanced economies with excellent scientists and both spend a relatively high proportion of their GDP on R&D — ranking fourth and fifth in the world, based on 1994 figures. Predictably, given their size and their investment in science, they also rank fourth and fifth in the number of scientific papers they produce.

Yet when it comes to the quality of those papers — as measured by the average number of times each paper is cited as a reference by subsequent researchers — their ranking slips to fourteenth (France) and fifteenth (Germany). They rank well behind the world leader, the USA, but also behind Switzerland, Sweden, Denmark, Britain and even behind Canada (seventh) and Australia (eighth).

Why? There could be a number of factors, but it is possible the answer may be that France and Germany are more committed to research institutes than the Anglo-Saxon and Scandinavian countries which conduct the bulk of their research in universities.

The peace and quiet of a research institute and the opportunity it provides to focus on a research mission, undistracted by teaching and other responsibilities may, after all, be a mixed blessing. It seems possible that the non-hierarchical nature of most North American and Northern European universities, coupled with the pervasive presence of irreverent undergraduate and postgraduate students could be an environment more conducive to productive research.

If this hypothesis is right, it has implications for Australia, which I gather has moved in recent decades toward more dedicated research centres, and even for Britain which is exploring a similar path.

Then there is another link in the chain: commercialisation of research. Advances at the level of pure science do not automatically translate into commercial or economic advantage for the discoverers. Again, there appear to be factors which allow some countries to seize such opportunities more readily than others.

These factors can include formal structures — like the availability of research funding at various stages of the process — but also informal influences like a national propensity for entrepreneurialism and risk taking. Even the attitudes of the popular press can play a part.

When it comes to creating commercially exploitable science-based products, there are three distinct phases.

The first stage is pure scientific research. This is research undertaken primarily for its own sake; to further understanding. While it is understood that this knowledge is useful and may well find some future commercial application, those commercial issues are not, at this point, the driving force. The important thing is to better understand the structures, processes or concepts involved.

An example of this is the early work on retro-viruses which was conducted before AIDS emerged, and was a matter of scientific interest only. Once the AIDS epidemic appeared, this work on retro-viruses greatly accelerated our understanding. The initial researchers didn't know where their work would be applied, but they did know that it was potentially important. That approach characterises much pure science.

The second phase, and the one that is often underrated, is the work needed just to determine whether a scientific discovery might have commercial extensions. This is a highly speculative investment because possible obstacles and potential rewards are, at this point, largely unknown. You are investing time and effort to determine whether this area of research even warrants further investment. From this can emerge a concept for a commercial product.

The third phase is bringing a costed proposal to a board for development of this commercial product. This is a more expensive and extensive phase but is based on an identified commercial goal.

All three phases are critical, but the funding requirements are different.

You need a solid investment in pure science just to get to the starting point — and this pure science tends to be funded largely by government or through philanthropic endowment. It is the pursuit of knowledge for its own sake, but it is also the basis from which much else flows.

However, if you want to see commercial rewards for your scientific advances, then for every dollar spent on the pure science phase, you need to spend $10 on the pre-commercialisation phase and $100 on preparing a formal commercialisation proposal.

It is these funding linkages that are often inadequately understood. Yes, you need governments to fund pure science research and you hope and expect that venture capitalists will fund the third stage, development of commercial products once the potential for these products has been clearly identified. But who funds the intermediate steps?

This risk is sometimes borne by academics themselves who may have to make a critical decision on whether to abandon a secure teaching/research career in order to commit a year or two to exploring a commercial concept which may or may not prove viable — albeit with the possibility of very substantial rewards if it is successful, but no guarantees that it will be.

This is the area where the US seems to have an advantage. There appear to be more academics willing to risk their own or their parents' funds to pursue this, and there are some business angels in the US who have made money out of some Silicon Valley venture and, rather than retiring to a country estate on the proceeds, are prepared to reinvest some of their profits in new pre-commercial studies in the hope of opening up a brand new field of investment.

It is a highly speculative investment because due diligence studies on risk and return do not exist — the funds are needed precisely to obtain the sort of knowledge which might make this possible.

Having spent some years as a director of research at Princeton before coming to Oxford I would venture an opinion — and it is a purely personal opinion based on observations in both countries — that social attitudes towards risk and failure might explain, at least in part, the greater availability of high-risk venture capital in the US. It appears to me that in the UK, and perhaps in Australia too, a person who has been a bankrupt is treated with some caution if they seek to raise funds for a new venture. In the US there appears to be a far wider acceptance that enterprise involves risk — and the fact that a person has had one commercial failure may be evidence of an entrepreneurial spirit and even a useful part of the learning experience, rather than some fatal character flaw which precludes them from further business life.

And what of Australia? Do we have the science base to be a player at the international table? Can this be a platform for knowledge-based industries?

Australia is generally a middle ranking science nation — not in the very topmost bracket, but certainly not in the bottom either. This is true of both our output and the funding we commit to science.

A 1997 study with which I was involved suggested that Australia's scientific output — as measured by the number of papers published in reputable peer-reviewed publications — placed it about eighth in the world. A further comparison, of the number of papers cited as references for other papers gave us a similar ranking — well behind the US, Switzerland, Sweden and Denmark, but ahead of countries like France, Germany and Japan. [See Table 1.]

That is a generalisation across the broad range of major disciplines, and Australia of course does better in some fields than others.

Using the measure of the number of times papers are cited by other researchers, Australia ranks in the top five nations in geosciences, environmental research, engineering and plant and animal sciences. [See Table 2.]

However, I'd offer one note of caution here: these studies reflect the past, not the future. The authors of papers included in these studies generally had their initial training perhaps twenty years ago, so it reflects the success of past policies more than current ones. Papers published over the past decade do not yet reflect the huge increase in education and science that has occurred in Asian countries like China, Korea, Singapore and Taiwan in recent years. The full fruits of this will not show up for a few years yet. The fact that our scientists are currently ranked in the mainstream of developed nations is thus not a cause for complacency.

Do we need more funding for universities?

Let me make a general observation, one that is not specific to Australia but to universities generally. I very much doubt that universities can significantly replace traditional forms of funding,

Table 1: World's top countries ranked by their share of the world's papers in science, medicine and engineering 1981–84.

Country	Share of papers %	Share of citations %	RCI	Ranking	% GDP spent on R&D
United States (US)	34.6	49.0	1.42	(1)	2.5
United Kingdom (UK)	8.0	9.1	1.14	(5)	2.2
Japan (JP)	7.3	5.7	0.78	(18)	2.9
Germany (GE)	7.0	6.0	0.86	(15)	2.3
France (FR)	5.2	4.5	0.87	(14)	2.4
Canada (CA)	4.5	4.5	1.0	(7)	1.6
Italy (IT)	2.7	2.1	0.75	(19)	1.2
India (IN)	2.4	0.7	0.27	(66)	0.7
Australia (AU)	2.1	2.1	0.97	(8)	1.6
Netherlands (NE)	2.0	2.2	1.10	(6)	1.9
Sweden (SE)	1.7	2.1	1.24	(3)	3.3
Switzerland (SW)	1.4	1.9	1.37	(2)	2.7
People's Republic of China (PR)	0.9	0.3	0.27	(65)	0.5
Denmark (DE)	0.8	1.0	1.16	(4)	1.8
Finland (FN)	0.7	0.6	0.9	(12)	2.4

Notes: Relative Citation Impact (RCI) is the average number of citations per paper. Expenditure as % of GDP is for 1994 except for Australia (1992) and Netherlands, Denmark and Sweden (1993).

Source: Science, vol. 275, 7 February, 1997.

Table 2: Comparative performance of scientific nations in different fields.

Field	Top five countries by total citations	Top five countries by RCI
Agriculture	US, JP, UK, CA, GE	SE, UK, DE, CA, NE
Astrophysics	US, UK, GE, FR, CA	US, SW, NE, CH, UK
Biology and biochemistry	US, UK, JP, GE, CA	US, SW, SE, UK, GE
Chemistry	US, JP, GE, UK, FR	US, SW, IS, NE, SE
Clinical medicine	US, UK, CA, GE, FR	US, CA, UK, SE, DE
Computer science	US, UK, CA, GE, FR	IS, US, SW, CA, DE
Ecology and environment	US, CA, UK, AU, GE	SE, NO, US, SW, AU
Engineering	US, UK, JP, GE, CA	DE, SE, US, SW, AU
Geosciences	US, UK, CA, FR, AU	US, AU, UK, SW, FR
Immunology	US, UK, FR, JP, GE	SW, US, BE, UK, SE
Material science	US, JP, GE, UK, FR	US, DE, NE, IS, SW
Mathematics	US, UK, FR, GE, CA	DE, NO, UK, US, NE
Macrobiology	US, UK, GE, JP, FR	US, SW, UK, NE, IS
Molecular biology and genetics	US, UK, GE, FR, JP	SW, UK, GE, UK, IS
Multidisciplinary	US, UK, USSR, FR, GE	US, SW, DE, SE, CA
Neuroscience	US, UK, CA, GE, FR	SE, US, SW, UK, DE
Pharmacology	US, UK, JP, GE, FR	SW, NZ, UK, US, SE
Physics	US, GE, JP, FR, UK	SW, DE, US, NE, IS
Plant and animal science	US, UK, CA, GE, AU	UK, SE, DE, US, AU
Psychology	US, UK, CA, AU, GE	US, SE, DE, UK, CA

Notes: RCI = relative citation impact (average no. of citations per paper).

See Table 1 for abbreviations; NO – Norway; IS – Israel; CH – Chile.

Source: Science, volume 275, 7 February 1997.

largely government funding, with profits from licensing their own technology or research outcomes. Profitability from the sale of technology licences is not a significant proportion of funding for universities anywhere. Even US universities draw a very modest proportion of funds from this source — less in fact than some British universities. The greater flow of non-government funding that US universities enjoy over their Australian counterparts is overwhelmingly due to the greater philanthropic tradition of the US and the tax laws that encourage this. So governments generally should not look to increased commercial activity by universities as a replacement for public funding.

There are a number of reasons why governments should invest in science — reasons that go further than just developing new technology to provide exports. That is important, but is by no means the only, or perhaps even the primary, goal.

Just as important is buying a place at the table of international science. Australia, with around 2 per cent of world GDP and a smaller proportion of the world's population, will inevitably produce only a modest proportion of the world's new technologies; the bulk of the new technology we use in the years ahead will have to be bought or adapted from elsewhere.

But to gain early access to that — before it has been widely adopted everywhere else, so robbing us of any advantage — we need to be players in the game. That is the only way we will have early warning of new developments; the only way we will be able to stay competitive. Unless we have a vigorous scientific community of our own, one that is capable of participating at a world level — making a contribution itself and fully understanding the contributions of others — we will not be in a position even to exploit international developments . . . unless we wait until they have been implemented by others.

Australia therefore needs to invest sufficiently in its science base to ensure that we are fully accepted, participating members of the global science community. Only that way will we be privy to the latest developments and be in a position to assess and implement them.

Beyond that there are broader, non-economic goals, that are equally important in their own way ... like contributing to the advancement of human knowledge and creating worthwhile opportunities for our bright young men and women.

There is also the matter of understanding the environment and our impact on it. But even with all the funding structures in place there is still another factor that can affect the pace and direction of scientific progress and that is public opinion. The public will not — and I would say *should* not — allow research to proceed unless it is confident that it is both safe and ethical.

The question is: Who drives the debate?

In Germany at the end of the 1980s public concern over the direction of biotechnology reached such a level that the government introduced restrictions on this research. Some of Germany's biggest (and most scientifically advanced) firms were forced to either halt such work or move it elsewhere. Subsequently there was a swing back in political attitudes and a reinvigoration of Germany's biotechnology industry has since occurred — but nonetheless considerable momentum was lost.

Now as someone who has done a lot of work in the environmental field, including studies on species extinction patterns, I share some of the concerns and reservations that many people have about possible impacts of the rapid commercialisation of science. As I pointed out in a paper on Science and Politics in July 2000 over and above all the utilitarian and self-interested reasons why humans should protect biodiversity, there is also an ethical, value-based argument that we have a duty of stewardship to the species with which we share this planet.

We need to be sure that we fully understand all the implications of what scientists are doing.

But even given that position, there are some grounds for reviewing the way decisions on these issues are reached. In the immediate aftermath of the BSE [often termed Mad Cow disease] outbreak in Britain in the 1990s — in which government ministers offered reassurances on safety that in some cases proved unfounded — much of the British media took up the issue of food safety. That led in many cases to campaigns against the introduction of genetically modified crops, dubbed by the media 'Frankenstein foods'.

This debate has certainly not been confined to Britain, but the UK experience has been extensively studied. In the highly competitive British media industry, none wanted to be left out and dispassionate reporting of the science was largely eclipsed by politically oriented campaigning.

A study of the debate concluded that all major radio and TV outlets and eight of the eleven major newspapers handled it in a campaigning rather than reporting fashion. Only 15 per cent of articles written on the issue were by specialist science correspondents and a host of various interest groups bought into the debate.

Now, I certainly share many of the concerns about the potential risks from genetic modification, but I would prefer to see debate about regulation of science covered in a rational way, rather than in an emotionally laden climate of sloganeering.

Creation of a proper forum for such debates is crucial to both the advancement of science and the protection of society. Because we are often operating at the very limits of current science, we will rarely have the benefit of perfect understanding, but we have an obligation to assess all the available views and information and to exercise sensible caution. We must at times admit uncertainty.

Even when that is done, and when real risks can be reasonably assessed, we have to acknowledge that people's subjective views and fears may not align with objective reality, and even though some scientists may consider such fears irrational, they need to be heard and considered in any genuine open debate. We need to accept too that many people will bring other agendas to such debates.

But recognising all the difficulties of trying to conduct full and open debates on scientific issues — all the fears and all the interest groups that will buy in — I still believe they are outweighed by their trust-promoting benefits. And anyway, as I wrote elsewhere, the world that deferred to authority advised by confidential cabals has gone. I do not mourn its passing.

These debates are never going to be easy for all those reasons I have outlined, but we do need to see scientists more directly involved — and, as well as wanting to see the public understanding science better, we need scientists to better understand public opinion.

Currently, the Royal Society has embarked on a five-year program of consultation to help create frameworks for such debates.

What is clear is that if a country wants to stake out a position in areas like genetic engineering and bio-medicine it must address these issues. The science cannot proceed without social, political and legal guidelines and it is better that these be developed on the basis of informed and open discussion.

CHAPTER FIVE

Rupert Murdoch

Rupert Murdoch is probably — no, unquestionably — the world's most famous Australian. Which is ironic because he is not, of course, an Australian at all these days, having had to adopt US citizenship in 1985 to comply with sections of the US media ownership laws.

Nonetheless, few things trigger greater xenophobia among people than the thought that their media has passed into foreign ownership, so Rupert Murdoch's lifelong quest to build a global media empire has inevitably drawn attention to his origins. Consequently people who cannot name an Australian politician or even film star or sports figure can tell you that Rupert Murdoch is 'the Australian media magnate.'

That is unlikely to bother him, for though he now lives mostly in the US — where his business is headquartered — he talks of Australia as though it is still part of his life.

In a personal sense it is: he has family here and property here and his business roots are here — and when he wanted to groom his son Lachlan for business he did so here.

In a business sense, however, Australia is now only a small part of his life. His company may own the majority of Australia's daily newspapers, a useful slice of the pay-TV market and a film studio, but the revenues from all of this represent just a tiny percentage of his global business — commonly only 3 per cent or so.

That simple statistic explains why Rupert K. Murdoch is the most successful Australian business figure in history. Other Australians quoted in this book manage global business empires — and that is a remarkable achievement — but these are empires created by others over generations. Murdoch has created his own global empire in a single lifetime.

In scope it is remarkable. In the US it includes the vast Fox TV network and Twentieth Century-Fox film empires along with newspapers, magazines and publishing houses; in Britain it includes a large slice of the dominant pay-TV network Sky, venerable newspapers like *The Times* and *Sunday Times*, and mass circulation popular papers like the *Sun* and the *News of the World*. In Europe it includes cable and satellite TV networks and in Asia both newspapers (Hong Kong's influential *South China Morning Post*) and the vast Star satellite TV network which reaches much of the world's most populous continent. That list is not exhaustive and nobody would suggest it is final; the game is still being played out.

This vast empire had its origins in Adelaide in 1953 with a single, now defunct, evening newspaper.

Rupert Murdoch's father, Sir Keith Murdoch, had been a celebrated journalist who rose to be chief executive of Australia's biggest newspaper group, the Herald and Weekly Times Ltd. Keith groomed his son for a similar role, ensuring that while studying at Oxford the young man (who then exhibited Leftist political tendencies that his father found alarming) also had the opportunity to get some first-hand tutoring in the arts of newspaper management from successful Fleet Street practitioners. He learnt well and learnt fast.

Keith Murdoch was, however, only an executive with the Herald group, not a major shareholder, and with his death in 1952 any prospect of young Rupert Murdoch getting a dynastic ride into the executive ranks evaporated. Keith Murdoch's only personal media stakes of consequence were holdings in the *Courier Mail* in Queensland and in the *News*, Adelaide's modest evening newspaper. The family sold the former but kept the latter and it was sufficient to give Rupert Murdoch an opportunity to demonstrate his management flair. He aggressively built up the *News* and used the proceeds to acquire other Australian newspapers, starting with Perth's *Sunday Times*, founding Australia's first national daily, *The Australian* and then buying the *Daily* and *Sunday Telegraph* in Sydney. Audaciously, he then repeated the tactics overseas — beginning with London's *News of the World*.

The *News*, the Adelaide paper which was the foundation of all this, no longer survives; (Murdoch was required to sell it under anti-monopoly rules when he bought the Herald and Weekly Times in 1987, but a few years later it ceased publication anyway, succumbing to the pressures which afflicted evening newspapers everywhere). Its enduring legacy is the title it gave to Murdoch's now-global business empire: News Corporation.

Rupert Murdoch swiftly realised that TV in all its various forms (free to air, cable and satellite) was the area with growth potential and over the years he has built up a global electronic network that now includes on-line activities. He has done so through both start-ups and acquisitions — and some of the acquisitions have been breathtaking in their scope.

Vast though it now is, News Corporation remains a work in progress, constantly adapting to changes in technologies or economic conditions — or simply to opportunity. Murdoch is continually exploring new opportunities for takeovers or mergers.

One such set of negotiations (worth US$50 billion, according to some media reports) had reached a critical point on the day Murdoch had earlier appointed to discuss this project at News Corporation's headquarters on Sixth Avenue, New York.

That is significant for several reasons. First it revealed Murdoch's remarkable emotional control: he emerged directly from these discussions — which from all accounts might have transformed the News empire but had ended in deadlock — and gave the question of Australia's future his (apparent) undivided attention.

Second it provided an opportunity to demonstrate his legendary candour. Less than an hour into our discussion (we talked in his office, but over a small coffee table) his PA interrupted to suggest that there was a call on the line he should take. It clearly related to the earlier talks. When I offered to leave the room Murdoch simply said: 'No, please stay if you want, but could you turn off the tape.' I did not feel comfortabe about remaining in the room and opted to wait in an adjoining office, but those who have worked with him say it is typical of his candour; that he tries to be as open as possible.

The discussion also demonstrated another aspect of Murdoch's character. Here is a man who has never hesitated to take a calculated business risk even when (as has happened several times) the outlay is so huge that it puts the whole News empire at risk if Murdoch fails to make the acquisition work in the manner he envisages. Sometimes it takes all his persuasive powers to convince financial markets that it can be pulled off, but his own nerve never seems to falter.

Yet personally he dislikes gambling — or gambling that relies on random chance rather than endeavour. He talks with apparent sincerity of his sadness at the explosive growth of gambling in Australia in recent decades and the social consequences that flow from it. He regrets that the hunger of governments for greater tax revenues leads them to encourage this rather than resist. At such moments it is easy to feel that he carries the legacy of his paternal grandfather, the Reverend Patrick John Murdoch, a Scots Free Church preacher.

It is also easy to understand the enigma he represents to many Britons who contrast his expressed personal values with the racy tabloids his company publishes there.

He is an enigma in other ways too. He was born in 1931 and has spent more than 50 years involved almost incessantly in intense media battles (many of which must have been mentally and emotionally exhausting). In his seventies, and with a new young family, he could be forgiven for seeking stability and security rather than pushing new boundaries. Instead the pace of business acquisitions and development is as intense as ever.

That approach is reflected in the discussions for this book. Rupert Murdoch's thoughtful and measured delivery never quite conceals his enthusiasm for the future — for the way education and science are transforming the world and creating new forms of social and economic wealth; for the extraordinary economic growth that is occurring in China and elsewhere in Asia; for the challenges and opportunities all these changes present for Australia.

He is not necessarily optimistic that we are taking all the required steps to grasp these opportunities, nor naïve in believing that there are easy pickings to be had in a globalised economy. There is, however, a real sense that the prizes are there to be won if we are prepared to chase them — and that, more than anything else, is the lesson of his own life.

Human capital is the key

There are two critical issues for Australia: immigration and education. The key to the future of any country today is not its physical resources or industrial capital; rather, it is human capital that will fund the health and the growth of nations in the years ahead.

While financial capital is a measure of present and past success, human capital represents potential for the future. The brains, the skills and the entrepreneurial spirit of its citizens are a country's most precious and powerful asset. The impressiveness of the Industrial Revolution that spread from Europe and the Digital Revolution that has spread all over the world have fooled us into valuing industries and technologies over the people who run them.

We need to think differently. We must realise that the financial assets of any country — its real estate, stocks, bonds, natural resources, pension fund reserves, cash deposits and other instruments — together comprise less than 30 per cent of the national balance sheet. Most of the rest is human capital — people.

By that measure Asia, not America, is the emerging superpower and by the same measure we can conclude that one of the world's greatest transfers of capital has been the migration, over the past decade, of nearly one million people from Russia to Israel, Europe and the US: a transaction that can be valued at close to one trillion Australian dollars.

So, if we consider people and the energy they generate is the key to real wealth and influence, then one of the big limitations on Australia is that there simply aren't enough of us.

We should have been far more aggressive in our approach to immigration. I'm not being critical of people for not having brought in unlimited numbers of refugees or whatever, but we should have been bringing in human capital on a far, far greater scale. We've missed some wonderful opportunities: Canada took in large numbers of Chinese before the handover of Hong Kong and at other times we could have taken more people from Europe.

There could be more opportunities yet. If we get another world recession there may be other opportunities, situations where people are looking to move. We should grasp those opportunities.

There aren't enough of us and we're a long way from most of the world's major economic centres. If we take an insular view of the world, and particularly of Asia, then there's a real danger that Australia will become marginalised.

That possibility worries me because I'm very fond of Australia and I've very deep roots there. I think that the lifestyle that's offered there and the opportunities are just as great as those in America.

We can't turn our back on Asia. We can say we're a European country in Asia, or we can say we're a multicultural European-based type country in Asia, and all that is totally acceptable. But we *are* part of Asia, which happens to contain 60 per cent of the world's population (or more, it depends on how you count Asia) — and they are people with basically great family values, great ability to study, and most of them are highly entrepreneurial in their outlook, their personal outlook on life. We should be tapping more of that.

So, I think we need more people. But most of all we need — even to the point of starving other services — much greater expenditure on education, though it has to be education of a type, particularly secondary and tertiary education.

We ought to be ensuring that our universities have the money to buy the best brains in the world — the best teachers and the best researchers, who in turn will draw the best students in the world. We can't do that across every discipline, of course, but you can choose a discipline which may be useful. Those people who then come from around the world to study at the university and to work there, some are going to stay, marry, have children, set up businesses, create opportunities.

You've only got to look at California, Northern California. Look at Stanford University, and the impact of its presence there — and Berkeley isn't insignificant either.

Stanford has spawned Silicon Valley and the whole high-tech industry. That high-tech economy is largely due to the fact that there's this wonderful, fantastically endowed university which has been operating there for the last 80 or 100 years, right through the last century. It produces wonderful graduates, who stay, and live next door, virtually, to the university. Many of the world's great companies are located there too, because that is where the bright researchers are and where the research that spawns start-up companies is emanating from.

Why is that? Several decades ago in California, a faculty member named Frederick Terman in Stanford's electrical engineering department convinced the American government to invest in the university and its research in electronics.

Today California's economy is the largest in the US, the fifth-largest in the world. Its university-based electronics industry is responsible for the region's economic renaissance, for the worldwide popularity of its colleges and — as any of us with a personal computer can attest — for much more than that.

And though California is a prime example, it is certainly not the only one. Look at Boston, the centre of higher education in America and now, as a direct consequence, one of the greatest centres of medical research in the world, with huge specialist hospitals and clinics. It is a huge employer of highly skilled people, and highly paid people.

We have to build our educational resources — our human wealth. We used to think a nation's wealth was the mountains of bauxite, or coal, or the oil off the coast. That is relatively meaningless: unless you've got special uses for it, you just sell it to someone else to work with. Not great. It is the knowledge-based industries that are creating the new wealth today. Look what wealth has been created in the computer chip industry and that's only playing with bits of sand and silicon. And now they are going to do it with carbon.

In Australia we don't have great companies that are based on that sort of intellectual capital — or none that come to mind, none that you could relate closely to knowledge industries. There's a handful of tiny biotech companies in Australia, but thousands of them in this country (the US). A percentage of those small US companies will go broke, but that's all right. That's entrepreneurialism. Some will survive and become important knowledge-based companies.

In Australia we have wonderful people, wonderfully creative people, but I don't think that we're really tapping their true potential and we're not doing enough to get more people to get these things going in the future And our tax laws — particularly, the execution of those laws — are a tremendous drag on entrepreneurship.

I think the educational establishment with its insistence on tenure at a tertiary level, and its power at primary and secondary level — setting bullshit syllabuses — is really doing the country an immense disservice. And I don't think we have politicians in either major party prepared to take that on.

Good universities can be great catalysts for their communities. I've talked about Silicon Valley and about Boston, but there's also Austin, Texas. That is a very good example. Out of the University of Texas came a young man, a young Texan called Michael Dell, who started a business nearby — and he's now the biggest maker of computers in America. He's only 39 or thereabouts, his company has a turnover of billions. It is employing many, many thousands of people. He's got a research campus of his own, everything.

I can't think of anything equivalent in Australia — no university that is capable of spawning an industry — but I suspect that with imagination and courage, it could be done.

Take Adelaide: it used to have a pretty good medical school but we should have built on it. They should have said: 'Look, we want this discipline, or that discipline.' They should have found the world's leading researchers in that discipline and offered them a million dollars a year to come to Adelaide and then another five million to get started, to recruit their best team. Some of them would have said 'okay, great lifestyle, great everything,' and agreed to come.

Then we'd have students from all over Australia — and then gradually from other parts of the world — all wanting to go to Adelaide to study those particular disciplines. We'd create a centre of genuine excellence that would attract people who would study there, stay on to work there and provide the base for a biomedical industry.

I remember talking to a few State politicians about this years ago and they'd just look at me and gasp: How could you pay a teacher a million dollars? I mean, the precedent was $75 000 or so in those days. But they do it here in the US.

By improving Australia's colleges and universities, our best generators of human capital, these institutions of higher education have the capacity both to develop the strengths of our own citizens and to attract a wealth of human power from elsewhere. The result would be a powerful diversity, a rich influx and output of skilled effort, that this country now lacks.

What has emerged in the last 50 years is international competition for human capital: a 'brain drain' from countries that don't have top-notch institutions of higher education and a growing pool of talent and value in countries that do. The US now has more than half a million students from other countries attending its universities, bringing with them a wealth of international knowledge and earning power. Australia, I think, has fewer than a hundred thousand. Nearly three-quarters of all Asian doctoral students in the sciences travel to the US for their graduate studies, and many make their lives there: a tremendous transfer of human capital. Meanwhile, in Australia, applications from postgraduate students — both foreign and Australian — declined in the first year of the new millennium, I'm told.

Without urgent support for our centres of learning, Australia is at risk of becoming something worse than globally disadvantaged: we risk global irrelevance. We need to accelerate the development of centres of real excellence in Australia. That is something the US seems to have done better even than countries like Britain.

A newspaper article in London a few months ago listed various diseases and the longevity of patients after being diagnosed with them in various countries. Britain was almost the bottom of the league everywhere.

I went to my doctor and asked if this is true? He said yes — 'because we don't have centres of excellence in Britain.' In America you go to New York, or Washington or Boston, you go to the major hospitals there and you will get experts on the narrowest of diseases. Whereas in Britain — and I guess to a lesser extent this is true in Australia — you go in for a cancer operation say of the colon, you'll get the cancer surgeon who's going to do a couple of colon operations but probably a lot of other things as well. A good all-rounder but it's not the same thing.

US universities also seem to forge closer links with industry than their Australian counterparts.

I'm not sufficiently expert on that subject to say that is so. There is no question that in this country [USA], universities love to be close to industries: they're a source of income, they're a source of students and in return the universities provide a source of skills and employees. Sometimes it takes the form of fairly formal relationships, more often it is a de facto situation.

You talked of closer links with Asia — as a source of migrants or as business partners?

I think the more that we can integrate — and there are limits to that — but the more that we can integrate with those countries and particularly with their industries, the more influence we'll have and the better off both sides will be.

The Asians, whether it be Chinese or Japanese, are still pouring into this country [the US] somehow or other, legally or illegally. Then we get a second generation, and you know, we discriminate against them. It is sort of unofficial — what was official is now unofficial in that you have to overcompensate the African-American population. But if you really opened it up totally to the best, I think Asians would fill 80 per cent of the top universities here. Look at the high schools in New York, you look at the school results, the dux of the school year after year, they're Asians and they're a fairly small part of the population compared to the African-Americans, the Mexicans, a whole lot. But that's Asians generally.

You've operated in both China and India, do you see both of those as having equal investment potential or is one more difficult than the other?

I would say getting started in business in China is more difficult, a lot more time consuming, but if you look forward, 40, 50 years there is probably much, much greater potential in China. India has so many divisions and difficulties — but equally India does have enormous potential. The trouble is, of their population of something like a billion, there'll be perhaps 60 per cent not really in the modern economy. They operate in almost a barter economy. There's poverty and even hunger in many areas. I find it a very depressing country at times for those reasons: you come face to face with the most gripping poverty. The only thing that seems to excite them is religious differences.

The Chinese on the other hand seem to hold together — they're a very interesting people, very different — but when it comes to certain matters of very basic economics like food or jobs or feelings of being ripped off by corrupt officials, people will take the law into their own hands. They are quite prepared to be violent.

You go to Bombay and you see people sleeping on the streets

who work in pretty basic jobs and they're cleaning their teeth in the gutters. And they think that they're okay because they are infinitely richer than they were in the countryside from where they've come, and they probably are. I think if I were one of them I'd be thinking of some sort of direct action to stir it up. But they have this kind of karma and accept pretty terrible conditions.

The truth of the matter is, China is making unbelievable advances.

India on the other hand is improving and growing and although corrupt, it is a functional democracy. Despite that, it can still be very, very difficult. Being a functional democracy, you can reach the politicians, you can talk to them, you can get promises but only seldom do you get any action.

In China it is very hard to reach government; if you do, it's very hard to get a positive answer, but when you get one, you've got it, you know where you stand.

But the most amazing thing about China is: people forget that only fifteen years ago in most of the big cities of China — perhaps not Shanghai, but most others — there was an unbelievably lower standard of living than there is today. There was food rationing — a kilo of meat a month. There was hardly a refrigerator in some cities fifteen years ago, where now there's a refrigerator and washing machine in almost every house. With living conditions they've come a long way in much of China.

If you go out west into the very poor provinces, among the peasantry, there is still great poverty and great resentment. For a non-Chinese it is very hard to tell how deep that resentment is and what they are going to do. In the past Chinese governments have always been changed by peasant uprisings. I wouldn't expect it now.

I think that they are moving forward. The leadership of China, above all else, is concerned about keeping the country together.

It can be very hard to generalise about China because it goes forward a bit, back a bit. But overall, I would be pretty optimistic about China, at least in terms of the Chinese people and the kind of life they're going to have. How democratic will it become? I think slowly, but it has come quite a long way. They're just very, very tough people and they are very intelligent.

And energetic?

Oh, unbelievable workers, yes. And the Indians too, work very hard. The Indians are great traders but you know, they leave India if they can. You'd see them in Britain: they take over the corner newsagency business and just run a small shop with the family living upstairs. They might have another existing newsagent nearby, but by law the newspaper companies must supply them with papers. They would start with the bare bones of a shop — stocking papers, cigarettes, candy and so on — but open 24 hours a day; whereas the English fellow down the road would open for a fairly resentful eight hours. Of course the Indians before long put him out of business. And a few years later they would have several shops and a few years later they would have a Rolls Royce and live in Wimbledon, and their children would be going to good schools. They've done incredibly well. I think it's true to say that, with individual exceptions, they've been very good migrants and melded in very well. You see them now in the House of Lords.

But I think Britain made a great mistake in denying British citizenship to the Hong Kong Chinese before the handover — the British were terrified they might all want to go there. They could have set tests or done something. We could have done a lot more in Australia.

You think we could be more aggressive still in taking in Asian migrants, or a good deal of the entrepreneurial ones?

Yes, I think so. We've had a lot in and I hope we have more — let's by all means encourage the best of them.

But not only them. We can get good people from other countries too. Things are not that great in parts of Britain — there's many people there who would make great, great migrants who can already speak the language etc. People are more mobile these days; they're prepared to move to further their career.

It is no big deal to go to Australia and get a job if you're an American, and if you decide to stay there and marry and settle down and so on you can do very well — just as it's no big deal now for Australians to come to the US or Britain. You get more melding of the English-speaking nations.

In the US you have this nonsense about dual languages and so on. It has to stop: you have to teach everyone English. It is not fair in California, if you go through school there where they speak only Spanish and you leave fluent in Spanish but not in English. They finally got a referendum on it and it was voted out — seven to three I think, I'm not entirely sure of the figure — but 60 per cent of the Mexican population voted against it continuing, because they knew that their children were not going to make it in this world if they couldn't speak good English. It's as simple as that. It might have been easier for them to learn the first year or two because instruction was in Spanish, but in the long term it was harming them.

There's also an issue of social cohesion.

In Australia we have a short history and we have within that history quite a lot of mythology. We have this wonderful love of the countryside or the bush as we call it, which I certainly share. In other countries, if you love space, very often you've go to go further to find it. In Britain you can't find it.

But somehow, let's facc it, we haven't got a glorious history; a binding experience of common struggle and achievement that shapes our identity. Australia's is not a bad history. We were part of the British Empire. We were brought up to believe we were British and to answer to the British flag when we went to war. In the Boer War or the First or Second War and so on, we automatically went to the war for Britain. We haven't got the history that this country [the US] has — the War of Independence, then a dreadful civil war, which settled an awful matter, but it does give tremendous heroes, a tremendous history and pride.

In Australia, we take pride in our past and in our pioneering, but it's more like the settling of the bush. There's an idolisation of the bush, which I find very easy to go along with, but it is not a genuine replacement of a prideful history.

Earlier you mentioned the tax system, and its negative effect on entrepreneurialism. Which element of the system — capital gains tax?

Capital gains, company tax, the progressive income tax. I think all the taxes are too high. Government is just too big — all government, state and federal. I'm not arguing for weak government by any means — quite the contrary — but I would be generally arguing for smaller government.

I take a somewhat libertarian view of these matters and I think the Australian mood, the mood of the average Australian, would be very similar. There is a tendency by not only the public service, but of politicians to forever be looking for new forms of taxation, new ways to raise more money to be spent in the ways that they think is best, but which I think might be more wisely spent by the people who have earned it.

I think one of the more distressing sights in Australia — and in the United States — is the tremendous rise in the number of casinos and legal gambling outlets generating tax revenues. Look at the spread of poker machines by parliaments of Australia and the money they raise . . . it is not a progressive tax, it's a regressive tax on poor people. It makes publicans rich, and it makes State governments rich, and what the hell do they do with it?

The lowering of barriers to international trade and investment: is that a positive for Australia?

Absolutely! I think this move of the present government trying to get a free trade area with America is absolutely right. There are a few things that it could stumble on, but I would suspect that its biggest problem is to get the attention of people in Washington. You know, we're a long way away, we're not in America's sphere of influence, not like Latin America.

In principle, they'll say yes, and then they'll say, 'Wait a minute; what about my sugar beet farmers in Montana?' and you'll say okay, you'll make an exception of them and then there will be something else — but it could possibly be done if they could just concentrate on it for 48 hours. It could be very good for Australia and then we could pull New Zealand in behind it; it could be very, very good, but I'm not counting any chickens just yet.

I know we're optimistic. But — how can I say it? — I think it's a problem of perception. Australians often feel the tyranny of distance, but now with the internet, long-distance telephone calls and the like, it's not intellectually any distance. But in perception it is. Whenever I go back to Australia, one of the first questions they ask me is: 'What do they think about us? What have they got in the papers about us in New York?' And I have to say, 'I'm sorry they don't think about us much. They're friendly and nice and they're aware of us and all that, but we're not on their minds much.' Mexico is, or Russia is, or you know, their local football team is.'

We do have a slight inferiority complex about that.

Which brings me back to my initial comment. We need more people, more human and intellectual capital, if we are to have relevance in our region and the world. That is why education and immigration should be our priorities.

CHAPTER SIX

Geoff Bible

Geoffrey C. Bible was, until he stepped down in August 2002, both CEO and Chairman of the Board of the Philip Morris group of companies. That made him unquestioned supremo of an organisation that includes not merely the huge tobacco businesses of Philip Morris, but also the Kraft Foods Group (which in turn owns Nabisco), Miller Brewing, one of the world's half-dozen biggest brewers, and the Jacob-Suchard coffee and confectionery conglomerate. Collectively those brands make Philip Morris the biggest provider of packaged consumer goods in the world. In January 2003, Philip Morris changed its name to the Altria Group.

The statistics are mind-numbing. Sales are almost US$90 billion a year (around A$160 billion). Profits for the 2001 year were US$8.9 billion (A$16 billion). It operates in 150 countries and employs around 169 000 people.

Geoff Bible sat at the top of this mighty pyramid for eight years and was in the CEO's chair when he participated in this project.

He was appointed to the top job in 1994, but at that time the appointment must have seemed as much a burden as an honour: some of the company's major brands were under pressure from competitors and the group's tobacco business faced the threat of endless litigation, with damage claims so huge they seemed likely to threaten the company's survival. And the threat was not only financial. The constant assaults by tobacco critics and the publicity given to litigation claims sapped both the focus of executives and morale.

Despite these prodigious challenges, the company has prospered under Bible — notwithstanding (or perhaps because of) entering into legal settlements of mind-boggling magnitude. In recent years earnings per share have risen and the share price has proved more resilient than any would have expected.

Small wonder that Rupert Murdoch describes Geoff Bible to me as 'probably the best CEO in the US' for his skill in maintaining not just earnings but also corporate morale in such demanding circumstances. The mutual respect between the two is such that Bible is on the board of News Corporation and Murdoch in turn sits on the Philip Morris Board. It is also an open secret that BHP Billiton would have liked to lure Geoff Bible back to Australia.

So what sort of person is he?

Professionally Geoff Bible is a giant, but in the flesh he is slight; not small in a bustling Napoleonic sense, but a neat, trim figure. Dapper would be a good word, if it did not have overtones of fussiness.

He's also warm, not in a beaming, hand-gripping, salesman's way, but in the intensity of his interest in your questions and in the absence of strut. Alone among the CEOs interviewed he begins by confessing to an uncertainty about the pertinence of his thoughts on Australia's future.

Nor does he make any effort to awe you with his surroundings. Philip Morris occupies an entire skyscraper on Manhattan's Park Avenue (with another nearby housing subsidiary operations) yet when we meet he is not behind a vast mahogany desk (as executives are so often pictured in movies), but in a conventional small meeting room with conventional blondewood furniture. He sits beside you, not across the table, and swivels the chair to face you . . . it's as if we are two people chatting at a coffee bar. He does not need the props of power to give him presence, yet presence he undoubtedly has. The best explanation I can suggest is that it flows from his sense of engagement with both people and ideas.

He remarks wryly that he had a previous invitation to chart directions for Australia — at a speech in Washington where the guest of honour was to be visiting Australian Prime Minister John Howard. Unfortunately the presentation was scheduled for 11 September 2001. Needless to say, the speech was never delivered.

Geoff Bible was born in Sydney and trained as a chartered accountant.

Because he joined a tobacco company as a regional financial manager and rose to the top, there is an inevitable temptation to picture him as the ultimate bean-counter, a man who measures the world by the bottom line.

His record suggests otherwise. For example, he made his managerial reputation not in tobacco but in humanitarian work with refugees. He worked for the United Nations Relief and Works Agency from 1959 to 1964 in Beirut, Damascus, Armenia and

Gaza, and the issue of how to alleviate the suffering of those people — or their descendants, many of whom are still in refugee camps 40 years later — still engages him. He has long been an active supporter of US welfare organisations, including serving on the board of the Committee for the Southern Poor and he talks openly about the impact that these experiences had on him. 'The level of poverty among some African-Americans in the south,' he says, 'I thought I could imagine it, but I couldn't, not until I saw it.'

What he does not talk about is the personal contribution he has made to alleviating such suffering. Charitable sources in the US say his personal gifts, particularly gifts to reduce homelessness, run to tens of millions of dollars. That is entirely separate from the US$125 million (around A$230 million) that the company gave in charitable donations last year.

He remains a regular attendee at his local parish church and is openly admiring of the vast amount of charitable work that fellow parishioners carry out and the funds they raise through community activities. Creating a more caring society is one of the goals to which he would like to see Australia committed.

His interests are diverse. He is a member of the Board of Directors of the New York Stock Exchange and also on the board of the Lincoln Center for the Performing Arts.

His rise within Philip Morris was brisk and continuous. Joining the company in 1969 as a financial and planning manager with responsibility for Europe, the Middle East and Africa, he soon became a vice president of Philip Morris International and then manager for Australia from 1981–83. He then returned to the US as President, Philip Morris International. He held a succession of ever more senior positions throughout the group — including President of Kraft General Foods — until his appointment as CEO and Chairman.

All this makes him hard to categorise. Within the company he is known for his awesome grasp of detail, yet his vision can be sweeping and imaginative. At critical times he has made televised presentations to staff around the world that even the most cynical have found reassuring, partly because he is willing to confront rather than gloss over difficulties. For a man trained in accounting and finance, his views on Australia are notable for the fact that he barely mentions things like corporate tax rates.

He says he can't offer any magic wand solutions to ensure Australia's economic future, and he even offers some gentle caution about the optimism of others. Then he gives real purpose to the discussion by talking about the Australian lifestyle in ways that make it seem worth fighting for. He then starts analysing the things that we can do well.

It is that combination of idealist and realist that makes Geoff Bible such a fascinating and stimulating individual. He can get you to look to the stars while keeping your feet on the ground.

>INTERVIEW

Open the doors and let prosperity flow in

Australia's future? I don't know: I've had views on this quite frequently — and I've tended to be wrong. Or the idea proves impractical.

I can give you an example. I was the honouree at the Australian American Association. You know the term honouree? The honouree is somebody from a company that has the greatest ability to put the arm on suppliers to raise the most money; it's as simple as that, believe me. However, one of the other functions is to make a speech.

The theme I planned for my speech was this: Having lived here in the US for a long time, what are a couple of things that appear to be important in America's success?

Number one, to me, is the open-armed approach the US tends to have towards people wanting to come here to start a new life — free from persecution, or just free from the inhibitions that you are under when trying to make a dollar in your own country.

You can come over to the US from Mexico where it can be pretty tough and here — well, at least here you get a shot. They get six dollars an hour, but they all work hard and save, and they move up a little bit. It is a bit like in Australia after the war. People would come over from Europe and they would buy a block of land, and they'd chop down the trees and put up a fibro garage and they'd live in the garage; they'd build a fibro house out at Blaxland or somewhere. It wasn't easy for them but their life was better than it was living in a tent, in a refugee camp in Europe after the war. And many of them did extraordinarily well and went on to make a real contribution to Australia.

I remember all that, so I feel very strongly about the concept of letting immigrants in — and Australia hasn't been all that great about that. For a long time now they've been pretty cautious about the numbers they'd take — and pre-1966 the White Australia Policy was in vogue and it was essentially only white people who could come and live in Australia. That changed in the sixties and now we have a lot of Asians coming in which is terrific.

But it is such a huge continent and so wealthy in its physical resources, you'd say Australia ought be able to do what America has done. In the US we're now nearly at three hundred million; the US economy is the engine of the world. There are things about America anybody can fault, but you'd have to say by and large, the system is terrific: just a phenomenal economy where people work extraordinarily hard, where there is a can-do type of attitude, where education still isn't as good as it ought to be, but it's still the best from the point of view of quality and availability, in my opinion.

So I had this great theory for my speech, about well, maybe Australia should open the floodgates and be more tolerant of immigration and give more immigrants encouragement.

Then two things happened. We read about the asylum seekers on the *Tampa* trying to illegally enter Australia and being turned back by John Howard — and that John Howard, who had been down in the polls, was suddenly rocketed to popularity because he'd resisted the arrival of 400 Afghans — rightly in my opinion because they are trying to arrive illegally and people are queuing up to get in legally. Nonetheless I thought a speech on Australian immigration at a time like that wasn't a very good idea. What I had intended as a comment on a long-term attitude to migration would have been seen as a direct political comment in the run-up to an election.

The other thing that happened was that terrorists crashed two planes into the World Trade Center and one into the Pentagon. That was 11 September 2001, the day I was to deliver my speech.

I was in a plane, on the runway at White Plains, New York, ready to take off for Washington when we were told to return immediately to the hangar. Obviously the whole function was called off.

Notwithstanding the timing, I still believe the points about migration and the lessons of a fairly open-door policy in the US are still relevant. I just don't know how you'd do it; how you'd get the policy accepted. None of the major political parties has embraced the idea — and they would be as aware as I am of the US experience — so you have to assume they see impediments. Perhaps given Australia's small population, it would be hard to bring in many more than you're bringing in currently.

But you look at this model here in the US, and you say, well, this was once a small population and they did it. How did they do it? Perhaps somebody should explore that, because it seems to have been an enormous generator of economic activity.

Somebody should be able to say, 'There is this approach that seems to have been an enormous dynamic for the US and here's Australia which is in some respects a photocopy of America — enormously wealthy in natural resources, terrific climate — why couldn't it work in Australia?'

So if I was looking to see what we could learn from the US experience, that would be one thing to study.

Another would be the charitable contributions and the tax

system and social attitudes which make them such a driving force in the community in the US.

The last figure I saw — I think it was for the year 2000 — US$203 billion dollars was given in charitable contributions in America. Now can you imagine how America would survive if that hadn't been given? Why is it given? It's not just that Americans are very generous people — the most generous in the world in my opinion — a lot of it is driven by favourable tax treatment. A lot of that giving is structured around the favourable treatment you get for charitable contributions and the creation of foundations.

America's need is great, of course. Australia doesn't have the poverty that you see in other countries. You don't see that many bums lying on the footpath or living in catacombs down around Central Station. You didn't in my day anyway, I guess you don't today, or not that I've seen on my visits back.

You do have poverty here in the US, particularly in parts of the South. I was on the board of the National Association for the Southern Poor, I'm no longer on it, but before I joined I had no idea of the level of poverty in the South. I thought I could imagine it, but I didn't. I had no conception. It is bad, very bad.

Nevertheless, a great deal is done, and a great deal is done through charitable contributions — two hundred and three billion dollars' worth, that's a lot of money.

Does that also reflect a different corporate culture; a different relationship between business and the community in the US compared to Australia?

Possibly. I'm probably not qualified to comment. We have a fairly sizeable business in Australia, in both food and tobacco and we give quite generously, but not on the scale we give here [in the US] I would suggest.

I used to think Australia was quite a charitable country. When I lived in Sydney, I'd get off the train of a morning and walk up Wynyard Station to work and, at least two mornings of the week, there'd be somebody there selling badges — Red Cross or Poppy Day or something. And you'd buy one — even if you were broke you'd buy one, because people were generally pretty generous. But the scale here is so phenomenal. There's more money and people are just more affluent generally.

There is a great sense of giving in the US and I think part of that arises — and this is just my own observation, and it may not be right — it arises from the fact that the country was settled by people who came here to avoid religious persecution and who probably therefore had charitable ideals. There is this strong sense in America of religious belief; that you look after your neighbour and you must share your good fortune with your neighbour. I think that is also prevalent in Australia, but I think it's more so here. I think church-going here is something you see more of than you see in Australia. I go to church every Sunday and the church is always full, no matter which one I go to — the five o'clock, or the seven o'clock, or the nine o'clock, or the twelve o'clock, they're always plenty full. And the plate seems to have plenty of money. The priest in my area distributes to charity all over the place; they have tremendous programs here.

I don't know the situation in Australia these days, but here the churches are dynamic. The guys are out there saying, 'Please leave your soup tins here for this cause, and those who can bake cookies on Monday for the Meals On Wheels over here, and those who can come and help us on Tuesday night, please come over here' — and boy, people roll up and do it.

That's probably a minor thing, but I think it's quite an important characteristic of a country, and that's a characteristic of this country that I think is important to its success. There is a strong emotional sense of loyalty, patriotism and help your neighbour, help the guy who's come in from Mexico, or Poland, or Russia or wherever, to kick off the new life.

It has been suggested that there is a philosophical difference here; that in Europe and Australia welfare and many other things that are cause for philanthropy here are considered a Government responsibility.

I think that's probably right, and I tell you what else: whilst you find government bureaucracies are bureaucracies everywhere, I feel that in the US there is a somewhat different attitude. They are more helpful; they are more, 'Let's get the job done.' They will strive to make your life — well, as least uncomfortable as possible, because going through a government process is nearly always an uncomfortable sort of experience — but they do seem to strive to try to make it work. In Australia I never have that feeling.

But going back to our original question about Australia and directions it might take, those are just a couple of basic elements that I think are important to a country. But maybe Australia is moving on the charitable contribution tax modification. I believe there's legislation.

On the immigration aspect, I don't know enough about it, other than to say, look, I would identify that as being a magical part of this country's [the USA's] success. Is there something we could learn from the model here?

A number of ministers have come through here over the years and said, 'You have big investments in Australia and we'd like to encourage you to invest more money in Australia . . . My answer is that I'd love to invest more money in Australia, but let me tell you how you see it sitting here. When I joined this company 33 years ago, we had a very small international cigarette business. Hardly anything in Europe, and Australia was its star. In fact Philip Morris Australia was one of the stars on the Australian stock exchange. We owned 72 per cent of the company then — in the 1980s — we've since bought the balance

Since then we've grown all around the world and Australia is still an important business to us, but it's probably now only about 1.5 per cent of the business. And no matter how hard we work to improve the profitability — and in the end you're in business to pay the shareholders a dividend; to run an efficient business, employ people and give money back to the shareholders — we can't seem to lift that. With the way the currency has moved, you bring the profit back here and you're lucky if you're standing still. So you make 100 million Aussie, and it becomes 50 US. Last year you made 90 million Aussie and it was 50 US, the year before we made 80 million Aussie and it was 50 US, and the year before that we made 50 Aussie it was 50 US. The currency has been on the downward slope for a while.

I was down there in 1981 running the Australian company, and it used to cost US$1.27 to buy one Aussie dollar. Today it costs you around 55 cents US to buy one Aussie dollar.

How can that happen to a country that's so wealthy? How can it devalue so dramatically? I mean, this last couple of years (2000–2001) has been unbelievable. South African currency's collapsed, 25 per cent, not unlike the Aussie dollar. But there's sort of a reason for it . . . you can see the issues. But Australia? I mean here's the rock of stability; great legislation, transparency, capital markets, terrific tourism, enormous exports — coal, natural gas, bauxite, iron ore, nickel, wheat, or meat . . . it is endless . . . And here we are devaluing: we've devalued against the Russian rouble! And the Russians — they've got a lot of problems.

So when I'm asked about investing further in Australia I have to say: 'Mr Minister, I'd love to find a good reason to invest, but there are difficulties.' Take our food business; we had fifteen cheese plants. It was an impossible situation so we restructured all that and got them down to a handful of more efficient plants. Cost us $100 million to restructure. We just had to get out of all this massive infrastructure we had acquired.

And you have difficult union conditions. We've come out of it okay, we've managed it quite well. But it is not easy.

There have been some improvements with the union situation of course. When I was in the tobacco company in Australia we had to deal with nine unions; it was complicated and we had some terrible strikes. We're now down to one and it is much better.

But as I was saying to this minister, if you take the food business, you've got a huge continent and distribution costs are disproportionate compared to most countries. The US is a big country, but you have volume to carry the cost of distribution. So the economics work against it a bit. In the tobacco industry we have so many regulations. Forget what one's views are on cigarettes, but cigarettes are a major industry. Here it's three million people; it's huge. The restrictions seem to be most demanding in English-speaking countries — if you take Australia, New Zealand, Canada, Ireland, Britain and America you have those who built the most ferocious attacks on the tobacco industry. And I think Australia is where it all emanated from. Those restrictions limit us from doing much more down there with tobacco.

Food is very difficult; if you look at what we are selling in Australia, in spreads like Vegemite and peanut spreads we have 85 per cent and 63 per cent of the market. We have 30 to 40 per cent of the cheese market, we're 40 to 50 per cent of salad dressings and mayonnaise. We just bought back our powdered soft drink business, Tang, and we just bought back our Maxwell House coffee trademark which had been sold years ago. But we have high market shares in 'mature' categories, I mean Vegemite, peanut butter, cheese, salad dressings. You can get more innovation going — super duper mayo, and Vegemite-plus or whatever — but there is not huge room for growth. Where do we go from here? Well, you can get into more commodity type things — and there are one or two things we're looking at — but it's hard to find a candidate for acquisition that would be sensible.

I'd like to invest more in Australia, I don't know where though. We had Lindemans Wine; we sold it because we found it was very hard to make money in wine in the conditions that existed then. That was a time when you had a huge surplus of wine and soft packs of it selling at four dollars for 4 litres. We were big in bottled wine. We had very good premium wines, and the soft pack took over, so we got out. Well, not long after we got out, the government introduced this scheme to pay growers to pull the vines out of the ground and they brought some order back to the wine industry and now of course it's going like a bullet because the Aussie dollar's come from US$1.27 to 50-something cents and that's helped enormously.

We were trying to sell wine here in the US at a time when every dollar it cost you in Australia was US$1.27. Breaking into the US market is tough any time because before they stock it the retailers ask, 'Could you tell me about your marketing program? How much are you going to spend on national advertising?' You've got to make a very big commitment, like 5 or 10 million dollars. That was hard when the exchange rate was so strongly against you and made Australian wine terribly expensive. With the Aussie dollar going down things are much better for wine here.

I think that the Australian monetary authorities must have figured out after the 1998 Asian financial crisis, that there's one way to dodge this bullet — let's take the Aussie dollar down — and they dodged it brilliantly, brilliantly. They were able to devalue without concurrent inflation — I don't know how they did it, but they did and it's magic.

Eight or nine years ago I used to think, 'I've got this thing finally sussed out. I know exactly how the world works, looking at it through the eyeglass of the currencies which are important.'

There were three strong currencies in the world once upon a time. It was the Swiss franc, the deutschmark and the yen. And the one thing those three countries have in common is they have no resources. None. So what have they got? I mean Switzerland has snow, and Japan has some snow and some fish, and Germany has a little bit of coal, That's it. And look at Australia, just rolling in all this stuff, rolling in it.

So, I asked myself, how come these countries with no resources are so strong? Well, they work, they work very hard and they're extremely well educated — the Japanese, the Swiss and the Germans were probably the best three in the world.

I thought, that's the solution: education and hard work will do it for you, you don't need resources — because look at Australia, flat broke! — it had the third-highest debt in the world. Not all of it was government debt; a fair bit of it was private debt — but still, the third-biggest debt in the world, something like 120 billion dollars.

So, that was my theory. Well that's all gone. Now, the yen's a disaster, Swiss franc's not doing great, the deutschmark has collapsed and the US dollar is flying high. So my theory doesn't work. It sounded pretty good though, I've got to tell you.

But there are things there that I think are still relevant.

Higher education, I think it is pretty good in Australia. Actually, I think it's very good, but what do you do to make it better? I was down there recently when Rupert Murdoch was there and he made this great speech about education. He's right about that ... education is the key and US higher education — particularly postgraduate education, is good; one of the country's strengths. It is probably the best in terms of quality and accessibility in the world.

Can you compare US and Australian education?

I think education in the US is still more available and it is pretty good, particularly the postgraduate stuff.

I think that the youngsters in the US, versus say Great Britain, come out of high school here slightly behind an A-level student in Britain. I think at university they nearly catch up, but postgraduate they catch up and pass. So there's a longer maturing process in this country, which is a great thing. I mean if you can afford to have a longer maturing process, I think it's just wonderful. You've got to grow up, but when you've got to be thirty-one at sixteen — in a sense of choosing your whole career direction — it's tough.

In Britain that's almost what you need to do because at A level you narrow it down to three subjects. They do seem more mature at that age in Britain. One of my daughters went to college here after being at boarding school in England and she was like ten years older than her classmates in maturity. The English boarding school gave her a tremendous sense of independence . . . an ability to not take drugs, and not binge-drink, that sort of stuff. She had a more mature attitude because she'd been in this independent jungle.

Where to now for Australia?

I think Australia has missed some marvellous opportunities. I don't know how they would've done this, but I think had we had more progressive thinking, 30 to 40 years ago, Sydney could be the Hong Kong of today, and we missed the boat. We had so much more going for us: we had good laws, understandable laws that work, we had transparency, skilled people, high education levels, good lawyers, good accountants, good business people. The tax system worked — terrific tax collectors; I'd say Australia and America were the two best tax countries in the world; very efficient. If you don't pay your taxes you go to jail. It works. You've got to pay your taxes or the country doesn't work — and Australians do pay their taxes so the country ought to work even better than it does.

There are some things that I think could've happened, but didn't happen. I'm not sure if they'd said to me, 'Okay Geoff, you're in charge of making Sydney the Hong Kong of the sixties,' I'm not sure I would know how to do it. But I think it would be possible to create conditions though tax or immigration initiatives.

There are opportunities. For example, we put in Melbourne our whole data centre for all of Asia. It services all of Asia including Japan, the whole thing is run from there. It is terrific. It could have been sited anywhere in Asia, but it is in Melbourne and it is working extremely well. In Australia you've got skilled people, commercially literate people and a sound legal system. You could go to court and sue somebody if they screwed it up. So it works for us and I think Australia could have had — still could have — much more of that.

I think from what little I've read about John Howard — and you don't get much news here — he's tried very hard to straighten out the industrial situation, and get better systems in place and have better relationships between employer and employee. I'm not opposed to unionism, I have to tell you; I think there is a place for proper unionism. The guy needs to have a place where he can go and complain. I'm all in favour of that, but it was being abused in Australia.

Do you see any advantage in Australia trying to join the North America Free Trade Agreement?

Yes, I think there's a chance of that. I talked to the President of Mexico last year and he told me something I hadn't realised: that Mexico has a trade deal with the EU and a free trade deal with the US. The opportunities that offers for triangular trade are just fantastic.

Then you've got trade blocs in South America and in Central America. If you link them — and that will happen in my opinion — you'll have a trade zone stretching from Canada down to Tierra del Fuego. That will happen. It will be phenomenal, and it will work, because these are people who aren't afraid of work. They're very good, decent hardworking people, who don't have much and who hunger for a lot.

I reckon there's a very good shot if Australia played their cards right, they could get into that. There'll be some troubling issues like meat, and wheat, and wool and so forth, but we ought be able to find a way through because the results would be terrific.

What we need in Australia is a big manufacturing base, but traditionally we don't do mass-manufacture efficiently and economically.

Is it a matter of volume, of economy of scale?

No, I think there's a bit more to it than that. I think Britain could've had the economies of scale, but they've shelved it. They couldn't do mass-manufacture efficiently — so motor cars largely went out the back door.

I think it's a question of mentality. I worry that Germany is going to demonstrate it can't be efficient in the way it was. I watched Germany twenty years ago and I watched our business there. The Germans still work hard, but the working week — the working year — has shrunk. The benefits have grown and German manufacturing has come off the boil. Then they swallowed East Germany, which wasn't a swallow of small proportions; it was like a snake swallowing an elephant and they will be paying the price of that for some time I fear.

I gather East German industry was fairly inefficient.

It was, but we bought a plant there and made it work.

I'll tell you a story as an aside now. I spent five years in the Middle East with the United Nations working with organisations for Palestinian refugees and I saw a lot of the problems there and I think about it all the time now. It drives me nuts. This thing has to be solved, and it's not being dealt with very well and the pity is, you've got all these people suffering miserably. Ninety-five per cent of the people are in misery and 5 per cent are the politicians and the terrorists and the fighters or whatever, running around with a gun. And these poor people in the middle living in mud huts or concrete shelters, have been there for 50 years — 54 years to be precise! Half of the first generation are probably dead now but their kids, and *their* kids are living in these same mud huts.

With no hope.

No hope. That's the key word, no hope. They've seen there is no hope. They've been there 50 years. It drives me nuts that we can't resolve a matter like that.

How is that relevant to Germany? We as a company went into a lot of the Soviet Union countries that collapsed — Kazakhstan, Lithuania, Ukraine, Russia, Hungary, Poland, the Czech republic. The existing plants there were not much more than bomb sites. Believe me, you wouldn't let your dog in it, most of them. We refurbished them, put in a beaut canteen, new uniforms, trained everybody, doubled their wages, did everything — and they all run like German clocks now. People were delighted, they're all fed, happy, they get benefits and our places are models, just models. We put a lot of money there, but we do very well. We do extremely well because we look after our people.

That gave me the idea that something similar could be done for the people of Palestine. If governments could create some sort of Palestinian State I was pretty sure you could develop incentives for companies like ours to set up there and establish modern, efficient facilities with decent working conditions that would create jobs and revenues. We could train the people in our other plants — just as we have trained people from Malaysia in our plant at Moorabbin in Victoria.

You can create jobs on a substantial scale. Look at Costa Rica.

Intel have built a fabulous plant there, it's purely an assembly plant and they do software kits. It represents something in the order of 30 per cent of Costa Rica's exports, and they employ around three thousand people. Now that's the sort of thing that could re-shape the place.

When it comes to Palestine and Gaza, I know the geography of the area reasonably well from when I worked there so I even thought I could map out what a Palestinian State might look like.

So I wrote out this letter to George W. Bush outlining all this.

Then when I finished I tore it up. I realised that he knows all of this; he knows he could help these people if a state was created and he's got people in the State Department who can draw him all the maps he needs. The hard part, the real obstacle, is getting all the people involved to accept any such plan. So it is no good telling the President what he should do if I can't tell him how to bring it about.

In a way that is relevant to my talking about Australia. It is one thing to talk about what it should do, another to find the ways to bring it about. That's often the hard part.

They know the problems down there. John Howard's a pretty basic practical bloke — he tells you pretty plainly how it is. And he loves Australia probably more than I do, I'm sure he loves Australia with a great passion, because he lives there and he has much more of a handle on what the problems are. I'm sure he and other leaders are familiar with the things I outline. Obviously there are obstacles to implementing them.

Our size and location are a problem: we're sort of a comma in the paragraph of the world aren't we?

I think muddling along as we are, we're doing quite well. I have to tell you, I go to Australia as I do every year, and I catch up with mates from when we were kids at school — six of them — and I always feel so much better. There must be something about going back to where you were born. I just feel terrific when I'm there. The sun's out, the light is lovely. It's a beautiful place, and it works like magic. Even the traffic flows, the restaurants are beautiful, the people are nice, the bush is superb, the motels are great, you can go anywhere with ease pretty well. It is a great life.

I ask myself: What are they doing wrong? Well, nothing, life's great. When you look at indices on a world scale of performance — particularly adjusting for currency values — Australia doesn't rate. But put that to one side. Look, if you're an Aussie, isn't life good? Your life is good. You don't bust your guts. It's Friday afternoon, nice bit of weather, I'll go for a sail. Life's pretty terrific; it's not over-taxed. Working conditions are pretty good, and housing is pretty good. There isn't that much poverty vis-à-vis what you see elsewhere in the world.

You don't have snow and cold winters and heating and all this maintenance you've got to do in the US, with your house collapsing and water crashing through the ceiling etc. You don't have that.

Higher education, we've got a terrific education system, skilled workforce.

So you say, 'What are we really worried about? Maybe we don't have a problem, maybe we're doing pretty well.'

I have one problem, I say to myself, the currency. Well if that's your only problem, it doesn't worry us, sitting here in Australia.

I'm not an economist, but one of Australia's enduring problems has been our current account deficit, made up of, I suppose the trade deficit or surplus and then the invisibles that go in and out, and direct investments and so forth.

I've lost track of the numbers, but from what I can gather, by and large we generally have a trade deficit of about a billion dollars a month, something like that. And you can't go on having that forever. I think that's what's causing the dollar to slide. And your interest bill is going up all the time. So you've got this deteriorating balance of payments and it's never got any better, it just gets worse.

It is in the same realm as Brazil and Argentina. They have a huge economy, but they're on the brink half the time. We have almost as much foreign debt as them — not government debt fortunately; a lot of it's private debt, which I think is more manageable than Argentina's.

So that's the difficulty we have to try to get to grips with: how do you reduce that almost constant debt. Well, we are exporting minerals and energy in a big way already and our agriculture is still competitive — but for me the area where we do extremely well, but where there really is more scope, is tourism.

Spain gets 50 million tourists a year — but they're geographically well located for the Germans, the English and several other countries. But if you think about it, Australia is such a beautiful place and 3 billion people live in Asia. Now okay, 2.4 billion of them are in India and China, and currently most of those don't have the money to come to Australia. But maybe they will, maybe they will. We've got to encourage that.

They say that India now has a middle class of 100 million people, or even 150 million.

Five years ago, we talked about there being 150 million affluent Indians for the purpose of buying various Philip Morris group products, so it's probably a bit more today. Over time you've got to say that more of these people will be in better shape — and you also have countries like Bangladesh, Pakistan, and others.

That, to me is probably the best hope. And maybe doing more, trying to encourage more of the things such as we have with our data centre there. Because Australia has those skills and a system that is transparent. The system works as in America, in France, in England . . . Australia is very efficient.

Jac Nasser thinks flexible Australian companies can find niche markets in a global market. Do you see that?

I'd like to hope so, but I haven't seen enough evidence yet of it happening on a significant enough scale. There are a few out there, but not a lot.

For me the best options — apart from the traditional industries — are still tourism and services like our data centre.

CHAPTER SEVEN

Leigh Clifford

Operations run by Rio Tinto, the company of which Leigh Clifford is CEO, produced in 2001 around $8 billion of exports for Australia. That is more than the total exports of our entire wool and wine industries combined.

That single fact alone would make his views on the future of Australia important. Rio is a major producer of coal, iron ore, bauxite-aluminium and gold — which just happen to be Australia's top four commodity exports. With minerals and energy supplying around 40 per cent of Australia's export earnings, it is difficult to do much economic crystal-ball-gazing for Australia without a perspective from that industry.

In that context Leigh Clifford is one of the powers in the industry that powers the Australian economy. But to suggest that he is here just to represent the minerals industry is to do him an injustice: He brings a much broader perspective — broader in a global sense, broader in the range of issues he has had to address.

Rio Tinto has major operations in North and South America, in Europe and in South-East Asia. Its operations include not just mining and energy but also aluminium smelting, and Leigh Clifford has at various times headed up operations in each of those divisions. These are all areas where international competition is fierce; they are essentially commodities, traded globally on a tariff-free and quota-free basis so that price and reliability of supply become the absolute basis of success. It is an industry where survival is dependent on efficiency — and Leigh Clifford was in management in Australia throughout a period when these markets became increasingly competitive. As a result he is widely remembered in some circles for being part of the management during the prolonged and sometimes bitter negotiations to change work practices, battles which frequently involved seeking more flexible and productive working arrangements in exchange for higher pay — offers which caused some rancour in the union movement as many employees moved from awards onto contracts. It was in some ways a watershed in Australian industrial relations.

It clearly left its mark on Leigh Clifford too. In his spacious office in London, looking out over the gardens of St James — almost an oasis of tranquillity in London's bustling West End — he talks of the sweep of issues facing Australia, but returns frequently to the theme that some Australians still have difficulty coming to terms with the realities of global competition.

He is youthful looking (he was born in 1947) and his manner is relaxed. Like several of the interviewees he at times talks as a father (he has two daughters) as much as a business figure; particularly when the conversation gets around to education where the experience of their own families gives much sharper focus to the relative merits of various international approaches.

He spent most of his working life with the Australian mining company CRA, a company in which Rio Tinto was a significant shareholder and which eventually merged with Rio. A graduate in engineering (followed by a Masters in engineering science) he held a series of executive positions in mining, energy and aluminium and became CEO of CRA in 1996. A year later, following its merger with Rio Tinto, he became CEO of Rio Tinto's energy division and subsequently moved to London. In 2000 he became CEO of the entire company, putting him in charge of assets totalling more than $25 billion worldwide.

Around 40 per cent of those assets are in Australia, so his home country still commands a fair bit of his attention, but it is now balanced by a wider outlook. At one stage the conversation turns to the relative quality of graduates from Australian, British and US universities and he quickly interposes that we should not think too narrowly in all this because 'we also see some outstanding graduates from Latin America.' He has become a truly global executive.

>INTERVIEW

Let's not fritter away our natural advantages

I am pleased to make whatever small contribution I can to this project because I do sometimes hear people whom I regard as out of touch with current issues in Australia pontificating about the situation there — and it does bother you to hear some of the things they say. It is reasonable for anybody to have an opinion, but sometimes the opinions — certainly some of the opinions delivered here in the UK — are based on information or perceptions that are not up to date and are unfortunately sometimes given greater credence than they deserve. So, as representative of a company with very significant and ongoing business operations in Australia I am willing to offer my perspective.

But even with that ongoing involvement with Australia and regular return visits, I don't keep track of all changes. I'd been based in London for two years or more when OneTel's troubles started making news and it struck me that I didn't really know much about the company or even know some of the key people involved. That was after less than two and a half years. So even though I'm in fairly constant touch and get back there pretty regularly, outside those areas that affect my industry there will still be changes in other areas that I haven't kept abreast of.

Does that distance also enable you to see some things in a broader context; to see global patterns?

Yes, and perhaps that OneTel example is a relevant one. There were some high-profile shareholders involved and to us, in Australia, it was quite big — but it's big in a smaller environment. The same thing was happening to similar companies in a lot of places.

But the collapse of some of these dot-coms and so-called tech stocks also gave the market a clearer indication of what benefits technology can and is delivering. When the so-called tech boom was at its height, analysts were always asking us: 'What's your e-business strategy?' I'd say we're going to use the internet — e-business if you like — to enhance our ability to produce metals and convince customers to buy them and to purchase goods and services. It's an extension of the telephone, the fax and email. It's a means to an end. I didn't ever believe we were going to have a new arm of business called e-business.

As a company, we invest heavily in research and technology in areas that affect our industry, but we don't need to reinvent the company to follow every technology that catches the market's attention. To sell iron ore, frankly, people transact administrative aspects of it across the internet but they don't make their decisions on purchasing large volumes of iron ore over the Net. I don't think they make the decision on purchasing high-value diamonds over the internet either. They like to look at that diamond personally under a good light. So while technology is creating some exciting new industries it isn't automatically making all existing industries superfluous — and in some cases it is enhancing the value of older industries by improving their efficiency.

That probably leads me to one of the core points of this discussion. People tend to ask what Australia is doing to prepare itself for this new environment where technology has a much enhanced capacity to create wealth.

I think we have got to be careful not to fall into the trap of trying to pick winners — 'Hey, I'm sorry mining and agriculture, you didn't make it to the list. What we want are dot-coms and biotechs, not farms and mines.'

Rather than trying to predict what particular businesses will flourish, I think we ought to be creating the right environment for business. If we get that right, enterprising individuals, companies and investors can find and exploit the opportunities in whatever field they may be in.

At the end of the day what we're talking about is how Australia can attract business investment — investment which ensures growth of opportunities for young people and generates income for the country.

If you look back at the late-nineteenth to early-twentieth century, Melbourne and Australia were very prosperous places. What were the criteria that enabled that prosperity? One was that institutions like law and government, although relatively young, were solid institutions. There was even an education system that was quite good for its time, and a work ethic. There was a fair degree of social cohesion. All of that was important for enabling business to proceed.

The other big element was an attractive environment for direct foreign investment — and because there was only a limited amount of local equity, it often *had* to be foreign investment.

At the moment there's a degree of terror, if you like, about the fact that, 'Gee we haven't got any global businesses headquartered in Australia.' But frankly 100 years or so ago we didn't have many global companies headquartered in Australia either, but we had prosperity, and we had jobs. What we had was direct foreign investment which is always better than debt.

Better in what way?

With any investment, there's an element of risk and it is better if the person or organisation making the investment is willing to carry that risk themselves. If there's an Australian willing to put up that capital, let's accept it by all means, but the size of the economy is such that some of these undertakings — be it the North West Shelf or whatever — are so big there sometimes just isn't the pool of available risk capital in Australia. So if someone else is willing to put risk capital in, there are still advantages for us. If it goes in as direct investment, rather than a loan, you don't have to repay it on the anniversary or pay the interest on it on the due date regardless of whether it is sufficiently profitable or not. And it doesn't move: direct investment is there. That's the point.

When you talk about overseas investment you hear people say: 'Yes, but what about the quality of job opportunities created?' I would suggest to you that Ford Motor Company and General Motors investments in Australia are pretty good quality investments. They've always been direct foreign investments, but I don't think anyone would suggest that the Holden engine plant and the design work associated with building Ford and Holden models here hasn't created quality jobs for Australians and given Australians a fair degree of expertise.

People raised various concerns when Rio and CRA joined to create the new Rio Tinto as a dual listed company (listed on the stock exchanges of both Britain and Australia), but with many head office functions now in London. But bear in mind, the investment that was CRA in the 1960s and 1970s, was what? — perhaps 90 per cent overseas owned? It was a foreign investment. Sure, it was Australian listed and there was some Australian equity, but the biggest proportion of the company was direct foreign investment and I'd suggest it produced quality jobs. Certainly for me as a young person I didn't feel the opportunities were limited because it was majority foreign owned. The development of Comalco, the development of Hamersley — all that was from a principally foreign owned company. They created a lot of good jobs — quality technical jobs for young people — a lot of taxes paid and a lot of goods and services bought.

I know we've side-tracked a bit, but the point I am making is that what is important is creating the environment for business to come in and do business in Australia. You want business that's socially responsible, that's environmentally acceptable and which pays fair wages and all that, but to attract those sorts of companies you need to create a sound business environment. Other people want that sort of investment too.

Governments — be they local, state or federal — have to recognise that they're in competition for these quality investments.

It is no good saying that people will want to come to Australia because Sydney's a great place to live — I have to tell you, when you look around the world there are a lot of good places to live. We have to recognise that our business environment, including our tax regimes have to be competitive

You can't say: 'Oh we don't need to worry about that; even if we are not financially attractive, companies will invest here because executives will want to live here.' They won't. I'm not saying

Sydney or Melbourne aren't great places, but the reality is there's a lot of American and European executives who think the quality of life where they come from is very attractive too.

What creates an attractive business environment?

Tax is of course one factor. The attractive places to invest in the world are tending to decrease their taxation rates. I'm not talking personal taxation — although there's an issue there about keeping bright young people living in Australia — I'm thinking more of corporate tax regimes. The managers of any company are entrusted with the savings of lots of people and they have an obligation to ensure a wise investment. They have a lot of investment opportunities and certainly the taxation regime can cause them to prefer to invest in one place compared to another. It is only one element of the investment decision, but one we need to be aware of. Most developed and developing countries are trying to create an environment to attract investments, so governments are in competition for investment.

To return to the point I made a moment ago, the role of governments is to create a climate for responsible investment, but it should not try to specify what that investment should be. It is the investor who puts up the money who should make that decision.

Everyone feels that the country should get into biotech and aerospace and silicon chips and so on, and I can understand that, but sometimes that's not your competitive advantage. Some very good business opportunities might be your strengths as a country. Investors will find good opportunities in whatever field may exist.

We have so many advantages as a nation — our good institutions, our social cohesion, a country free of corruption, a country free of violence. That nudges us in front of the pack: what we don't want to do is pull ourselves back to the pack with an over-restrictive regulatory regime — like some of the more onerous aspects of foreign investment restrictions that existed twenty years or so ago.

That brings me to the broader question of our place in a world in which trade barriers are generally falling.

There is a need for us, as a community, to recognise that globalisation has been going on for a long time. The expansion of trade has been a recurring event throughout much human history, rapidly accelerated at times by the establishment of empires. In that sense globalisation is a fact of life — despite occasional King Canute-like efforts by some people to stop it. [Canute was an Anglo-Saxon king who, according to legend, vainly attempted to order the incoming tide to recede.]

Interestingly, in this current debate much of the protest has been from people in the more developed world — largely Europe and the US. In general, it is not Mexicans out there saying they feel disadvantaged; it is people from across the border.

It's vital for us — and by us I mean the developed world — that globalisation proceeds, just as it is vital for developing countries. And I think the situation is that it's just a fact of life: it is happening and it will continue. Now I realise the adjustment that this involves can quite often be painful for individuals, when the industry or enterprise in which you work is no longer competitive and an adjustment occurs — but we've seen that if you don't make that adjustment the pain can be worse.

Globalisation is occurring and I think we can actually turn it to our advantage because we are basically a country which is now pretty free of barriers. So the pressure is going to be on others to enable their industries to be competitive — and you know, our agricultural and primary industries areas are competitive.

Resource development is one area in which Australia has really developed a world position.

Agreed. So, we don't put lead in our saddlebags by doing something absurd regarding energy. The reality is, we've been through a period of probably the best part of twenty plus years of relatively cheap world energy and energy's maybe going to get a little more expensive in future. Australia is a country with access to significant energy resources, including and gas and coal. Let's not rush in to disadvantage ourselves at a time when these things may well become more valuable.

One of the things I've noted is that respect for the environment and good environmental performance usually goes hand in hand with economic prosperity. That's my observation. It's the old hierarchy of needs issue; when you are desperately poor other things slip down your priority list.

I've had a fair bit of experience in Indonesia, and we are pretty proud of our operation there. Now you hear people raise various issues about mining in Indonesia; what they ought perhaps to be asking is about the 20 million people who live in Jakarta in appalling conditions — appalling sanitary, water and air standards. Our operations are idyllic compared to that.

Just an observation flowing from that: we tend to get almost over-reporting with things in Australia; we've got a hell of a lot of media for the amount of news generated. To give an example, we get here at head office in London regular clippings of what is written about Rio Tinto everywhere in the world. If we get two mentions in the rest of the world in a day, we get twenty in Australia. I'd be fairly certain we are not in the *Financial Times* today or whatever other paper is on the desk over there. Or if we are, it will say Rio Tinto went up 10p or down 10p. We're about the twenty-something largest company here. So we expect to be reported on from time to time. But in Australia we get a stack of clippings daily about what we are doing. Sometimes it seems that in Australia we are looking at our own little fishbowl too intently, so we know every fish in that fishbowl and we check their scales daily, rather than looking at some of the other fishbowls as well.

Perhaps the other aspect of that is that we in business haven't done a very good job selling to the community as a whole the importance of a vibrant growing business community and, where it sits in our society.

I was at a talk here the other day that Tony Blair gave and I got the impression he was rather more aware of these things than would be common in Australia. Now you can say he was talking to a largely business audience, but it wasn't just rolling off the tongue. They're a Labour Government, but it always seems to me that a government of either persuasion in this country sees business as absolutely critical to the prosperity and welfare of Britain and the British people. I'm not sure that a similar understanding exists in Australia.

I don't know how you achieve that. In a sense Britain is a trading nation and also a huge supplier of financial services; the City [London's financial centre] is vital to the prosperity of the UK. The British seem to know this and they know that they are going to be part of globalisation. People don't talk as though somehow or other, there's a choice.

I think we've got to recognise in Australia that there's no choice either.

State governments are probably closer to where the rubber hits the road as far as business goes and often they are more aware of the importance of a good business environment than their federal counterparts. I found it very interesting seeing an advertisement from Premier Beattie after his election saying Queensland was 'open for business'. That sort of thinking needs to pervade every government minister in every state and at federal level.

Charles Court did something similar for Western Australia years ago.

Yes, and as someone once said in Western Australia: 'We haven't had a slump in years, but this is the worst boom I can remember.' They're very conscious of business there.

I just get the sense that the importance of business — the big end of town as it's sometimes called — is something that government in Australia ought to be absolutely embracing; they ought to be embracing the little end of town, the smaller businesses too. At the end of the day, it's simply about encouraging people to invest so that we create opportunities and prosperity.

If you look at living standards around the world, they tend to be broadly correlated to the capital backing behind each worker. To a significant degree that's what distinguishes the richer countries from the poorer.

I'm not sure that that's inculcated into our education systems to the degree it ought to be. Is that the fault of business or is it the fault of the education system? I don't know.

There are elements of our society though, where I think there is a fairly sophisticated level of understanding. There are those in the union and labour movement for example who, while they have different responsibilities and represent a different constituency from me, do understand these economic fundamentals pretty well.

Over the years I've had a few talks with Martin Ferguson. I don't know him closely, and obviously we've not been on the same side at times, but I've found him very thoughtful about some of the issues and he's given me some very good advice. We used that advice — and I told him we used it. It was wise advice.

When you look at the labour movement — the union movement — particularly in the UK, they've moved on beyond what I'd call some of the old phases of the class struggle. I've seen some very interesting attitude changes as the auto industry here has gone through its restructuring. People have recognised that the UK's future does not lie in restrictions which put their manufacturing industry at a disadvantage. They also recognise that they're probably not going to be able to survive and prosper making only the little Ford Lasers; they've recognised that Jaguars and higher technology, higher value-added manufacturing is going to be the way. I have to say the union officials and some people I've talked to in the UK have moved on. They're now looking at what life's going to be like in the mid-twenty-first century. I'm not sure that everyone in Australia has moved the same way, although I've talked with Greg Combet and he's pretty alert too. But not everybody in the movement — certainly not as you go further down the hierarchy — is attuned to what's going on in the rest of the world.

Tony Blair and Britain's New Labour have certainly moved on from some of the Old Left agendas. I think that what you're seeing is a real recognition that globalisation is here to stay. The EU is about globalisation — or very extensive internationalisation — and debates about the euro and suchlike raise a lot of sovereign issues; issues of national control and identity. But I sense that these debates are conducted within an acceptance that globalisation is here and that Britain has to work in this framework. I think a lot of people in Australia actually haven't fully realised that yet and accepted that it means there are going to be changes, just as there were changes in the UK.

The reality is that the pace of change will probably accelerate, not decelerate, and change can be painful. Human nature is such that when you have gone through the pain of change once, you'd rather call a halt to it; rest for a bit. I remember a union leader once said to me when we were talking about the readjustment process: 'But didn't we do that last year? Haven't we done that?' — as though change and efficiency improvement was a one-off thing, not something we will have to address continuously to stay competitive.

I remember telling a union official once that 'a change is going to roll through this coal industry like you've never seen.' That was in 1986 and I am sure he thought the changes of the next few years were the changes I was talking about. They were just the start; the industry has made lot of further adjustment since then. It has had to.

The reality is that we're in competition in the energy business with all other suppliers and we've got to do what's necessary to stay there. There's not much quarter given or asked for out there. But we have some advantages in energy supply in Australia so we can compete.

That brings me back to my initial point which is that the role of governments is to create environments in which people can seize whatever opportunities exist. That is the key to our prosperity. Governments ought to create an environment of stability, create an environment of confidence about the taxation regime and create an education system which ensures that people are well educated because I think the days of poorly educated people being able to command worthwhile jobs are largely over.

What's your perception of the Australian education system? How good is it?

Just before I answer that, there are a couple of other points I should make about Australia generally. I think there's a good work ethic in Australia. People get on with the job and they work well in teams. They're actually quite accommodating of different cultures. They are adaptable, they get on with the job and they travel well. You find Australians in just about every corner of the globe in our industry — although you also find New Zealanders and Canadians, but Australians do seem to adapt pretty well.

As far as the education system goes, if you look at basic matriculation level education then Australian kids are well educated. Using the experiences of my own family who spent time in both the Australian and UK systems, the end results seem broadly comparable. There are differences of course: the UK system tends to be very narrow for the last couple of years; great depth, but quite narrow.

Our universities seem pretty competitive with most other countries too. As a company, we see graduates from many countries and the good ones from Australia can hold their own with those from the UK or US. And not just from there: we also see some outstanding graduates out of Latin America. But overall, I'd have to say that the education system in Australia meets the needs of business.

If you are asking about the quality of specific facilities in the universities, I don't have the detail. I get the sense from other conversations that basic capital investment in the universities in Australia is falling behind. But that's more a sense than an informed opinion and it is an issue for universities in the UK too when people contrast them with universities in the United States, some of which appear to be pretty well funded. That may have a lot to do with the basic wealth of the country, its history of philanthropy and the tax structures that encourage it.

They seem to be more generous, or the relationship between business and universities seems closer?

There is more technology-based industry in the US of course, which may lead to more interaction. But I'd have to say it would probably surprise you how much activity goes on with academics in Australia. It is a much smaller economy but there's interaction; certainly I've never found any lack of willingness for academics to work with the industry, if given the opportunity.

Much of this leads back, however, to the centrality of the point I made earlier: that if you have a vibrant investment and business climate that creates prosperity, much else flows from it.

When I look at Australia from this distance, I think we've got some tremendous strengths — basic societal strengths — which at times we probably don't recognise and what we've got to make sure is that we build on our strengths; that we don't do things which discourage people from investing there and running businesses there. If we do things right the investment will come.

Another, not totally unrelated issue, is that we've got to retain incentive for young people. Someone said to me the other day they wouldn't be surprised that UK and US firms would start to recruit lawyers direct from universities in Australia shortly. The best lawyers or engineers or doctors or dentists or whatever, in Australia will hold their own anywhere. We've seen that over time. Now young people tend to be footloose and to want to see the world, that's fine; it broadens their experience and outlook. But what we don't want is a situation where a bright young person says they'll stay overseas, not only because the money's a little bit better — on current exchange rates — but also because the taxation structure is such that it's not attractive to come home. We've got to watch that the top marginal tax rate isn't set at so low a threshold that it catches these people and makes moving permanently abroad seem attractive.

Look across the Tasman to New Zealand. There is a country that in my opinion has some tremendous challenges. It is a country with a good education system, lots of other attributes and yet young people are leaving in droves. Why? Some would say it's for opportunities, but I think if you put too much lead in their saddle-bags, they'll run on another track.

I'm not talking about myself or people in my position — it's not going to alter my lifestyle. It is the younger people we need to think of; the people who are struggling to pay off their mortgage and put their kids through school. Despite the changes we have made, we're taking too much off their margin.

What are the limitations of our size?

That's a significant issue. Some years ago a few of us in business got together to try to get increased immigration back on the agenda. There was me, Frank Lowy, Hugh Morgan, Fred Hilmer and a few others. One of the objectives was to get people to recognise that we were faced with the prospect of a country peaking at 23 million with an ageing population. Is that sustainable? For a while now large-scale immigration seems to have been something which is very difficult for any party to put forward as their platform, but we need to do something. What is our official intake? It was 80–90 000, or so and it is now maybe a bit higher, but Canada's is 250 000.

History has shown us that if you can choose the immigrants, you can get some damn good immigrants and I think it's something we ought to be doing. I think certainly it's been demonstrated that we are better off for the immigration that has occurred, and there are still people who want to come there who've got attributes we ought to be seeking.

We talked earlier of encouraging greater investment. Has compulsory superannuation helped there?

If you look at this from where I'm sitting, you can see the countries which have funded pension plans tend to have a more vibrant equity market and I think that's a good thing. Where pensions are unfunded, I think it's a less desirable situation. Undoubtedly in the US, where the pension plan system allows many people to make their own decisions, there's a pool of money available for investment and we've seen the US now start to look overseas more for investment . . .

I don't know what the flow of funds from compulsory superannuation is in Australia, but it would be substantial. I also think it's a prudent move to have people planning for their retirement and that's effectively what it is. But they need to watch that the tax regime on it doesn't undermine its attractiveness to some people.

Within the resources sector I get the impression that technology has increased the capacity to find minerals and therefore the critical issue now is to develop them efficiently. Is that so?

Well, maybe the capacity to find them has increased, but finding the really good ones isn't getting any easier. You don't stub your toe on an elephant [mining jargon for a big deposit] very often.

When you look at the surface of the earth, it would surprise you where the old explorers have been and where the new explorers have been. So the deposits you are now looking for are probably located beneath cover, so we've got to use more sophisticated techniques. Despite the technology, they're still pretty hard to find.

One of the things is that when you find something nowadays you're talking half a billion dollars to develop it for anything of substance, or a billion dollars to develop it. With that sort of commitment you want to be satisfied that the undertakings you are given before you proceed are binding. You need to have very secure agreements to commit that sort of money.

In our business we can't shut up shop and disassemble the plant; you can't take the hole elsewhere. Once we're there, we're there for the long haul. We've got the majority of our bigger businesses located in North America and Australia where there's respect for the rule of law. That is not to say we don't have some tremendous businesses elsewhere; we have, but it just so happens the majority of them are in those areas.

I think a very interesting place is Chile, which over a space of about twenty years has really made enormous advances. It is fair to say there was a time when Chile was in the bottom tier of countries in Latin America to invest, but in the last decade or so, Chile has been very stable in terms of its investment climate and respect for law. Chile is a very good place to do business. We're very comfortable with our major investment with BHP in Chile. I think other countries have looked at Chile and said, 'Hey, if you create the environment and you've got some attractive, well in their case, mineral terrain, you'll get investment.'

Is mineral exploration getting more expensive?

Exploration tends to be very technology intensive, but the best exploration tools are still the geologists' eye and the diamond drill. One of them is a unique commodity, the other one's a pretty expensive process. But as we said, finding things is only one half of the equation; the other is developing them. I can think of places in the world where there are some fabulous ore bodies that are known now and are probably still going to be there — still undeveloped — in twenty years time. And the reason they won't be developed is because of bureaucracy, lack of respect for law, political instability, lack of institutions.

In a broader sense, how is Australia regarded internationally?

When you are living outside a country — and in this role I have a lot of involvement with many countries; most major regions — it does give you a different perspective. We sometimes imagine in Australia that we are on the tip of everybody's tongue, or in their thoughts. The reality is we're not. We are 20 million or so people and an economy which is not insignificant, but the reality is, we're not on the tip of everyone's tongue and most of the investors, let's face it, are in North America, Europe or increasingly in parts of Asia. They have alternatives. They have options.

Sure we get some prominence out of our sporting stars, but

we're not constantly in the minds of everyone with regards to business opportunities. We probably punch above our 20 million, but that doesn't mean we can't do better.

It's very interesting to look at Ireland. It has made itself extremely attractive. Now I'm not sure if they said they want to target the particular changes they made — they probably did to some degree — but by God they've gone from being one of the basket case economies, to quite a success story; and part of it has been a very young well-educated workforce. I think Australia does have a good education system; education is available to all in Australia and they are capable of getting quality education through the universities and in general that is fairly readily available. I think the HECS system, where you can pay out of your subsequent earnings is a good system. Someone has to pay.

Speaking of tax systems, we have incentives for research, but the biggest commitment you make is the first commercial-scale plant using a new technology. What can be done about that?

Well, we're faced with that dilemma ourselves. Installing new technology in very expensive new plants is always a big decision and you have to decide where you are going to site that first plant.

You certainly don't want needless complications that add to price risk. I. have to say that's where the labour movement has to recognise that sometimes union leaders — and I'm not suggesting for a moment the most senior people; they recognise the importance of investment — but by God, lower down the union hierarchy they've got to understand that, stuff these things up and word spreads. People get very nervous about making big commitments. You mentioned before about the fact that you can find ore bodies, but the trick is bringing them to fruition. The reality is, in the United States your ability to construct major capital works is so much better. Until the last few years when they've had such a strong US dollar, they were extremely productive in construction and development. In Australia we've got to do everything to make sure our engineering capital cost is not impeded in any way, otherwise the burdens of our construction processes there can destroy the benefit of our other advantages.

Are you thinking in terms of regulatory environment or of industry practices?

The construction industry has gone through a considerable debate about industry practices — union bloody-mindedness at times, for want of a better description. Those things can't be tolerated because ultimately, they discourage people undertaking development projects. They affect everybody.

I'll been frank: we've looked at — and are looking at — investments, and one of the things I'm very conscious of is what I call construction productivity. Not about paying people poor wages, just about bloody-mindedness which occasionally has existed in the past. I hope what I've been hearing lately is not a version of the past.

Are Australian wage rates a significant factor?

Look, wage rates in Australia aren't the issue. Exchange rates go up and down and that affects wage rates in terms of international competitiveness, but by and large wage rates in Australia are not the issue. What is an issue is when you get absurd restrictions which don't appear to be related to genuine workplace issues but often seem just an attempt to sometimes demand something.

The phrase 'feather-bedding', I think it's basically gone out of the lexicon in Britain and it's not a bad thing, because people recognise you can't have that. I mean they've gone past that in the UK; there isn't that debate here about feather-bedding. It used to be rife in some industries in Britain — and what was the economic environment in the UK at the time? They went to hell and back in some industries here in Britain, but now there's a much more productive approach.

It all comes back to those fundamentals. We've got a stable society with a high level of harmony and tolerance. We've got democracy, the rule of law, sound education, a work ethic. These things should all give us an edge in developing whatever industries are in Australia. If we can avoid complicating things with needless restrictions, I think we can feel reasonably optimistic.

CHAPTER EIGHT

Rod Eddington

There's something disarmingly youthful about Rod Eddington. It is not just the physical appearance, though at 51 his face does not show much sign of the stresses of two decades of senior executive roles in a tough industry. No, the youthfulness is more in the manner; a boyish enthusiasm and a lack of cynicism. At first meeting it could almost be taken — by the tough standards of the corporate world — for a touch of naivety. You wonder how many commercial opponents have been lulled into underrating the strong intellect that lies behind it.

It was that intellect that first drew him away from the University of Western Australia, where he graduated in engineering, to

Oxford, courtesy of a Rhodes scholarship (where he was sandwiched between former Federal Labor leader Kim Beazley and current West Australian premier Geoff Gallop who respectively preceded and followed him there as Rhodes scholars). He was star quality even then. Media reports say fellow students nicknamed him God for his uncanny abilities, both academic and on the cricket field. These days he is uncomfortable with the reminder.

At the end of his scholarship he joined the teaching staff at Oxford until he was recruited by the Squire group, which sent him to Asia as an executive with Cathay Pacific airline. He became CEO of Cathay in 1992.

His sixteen years in Asia furnished him with both a wife and a conviction that Asia will be the theatre where Australia's future is largely shaped. He sees building stronger bridges with Asia and Asians as probably Australia's most urgent task.

He knocked back an approach to run Qantas in 1993, but three years later accepted an offer to head up its ailing rival Ansett. It was a daunting task since Ansett was loaded with debt, had an ageing and unnecessarily diverse fleet and carried a number of unrelated and unprofitable subsidiaries. Why accept the much tougher job with Ansett when he had already declined the plum position at Qantas? The answer, it was widely reported, lay in two words: Rupert Murdoch.

Murdoch's News Corporation then owned 50 per cent of Ansett and was desperately keen to either return the airline to profitability or exit it at a respectable price — or preferably both. It was News Corp which recruited Eddington and he delivered to them in spades. Within two years Ansett recorded a A$110 million annual profit and within four years Air New Zealand, which already owned half of Ansett, agreed to buy the balance from News.

That was in February 2000. In April Rod Eddington accepted an approach to run the very much larger British Airways (which in turn owns 25 per cent of Qantas). Ansett survived little more than eighteen months under Air New Zealand management.

The mutual respect Eddington and Murdoch shared as a result of that experience has endured and Eddington remains a member of the News Corporation board of directors. Indeed, there were many who were surprised that when he left Ansett, he went to British Airways. A senior job in Murdoch's empire was considered just as likely and probably more attractive.

Eddington was under no illusions that life at British Airways would be easy, for despite its size and prestige, it too was struggling in a hugely competitive market, but he had strategies for turning things around. Alas, no strategy could have accommodated the aftermath of the September 11 terrorist attacks. Airline passenger traffic everywhere nosedived and on the Atlantic route, so critical to BA, it plummeted. Within weeks British Airways (in common with other airlines) was losing millions of dollars a day. Worse, the slump in passenger traffic proved stubbornly prolonged. Months later several airlines around the world had folded, there was little sign of any dramatic turnaround and analysts were starting to talk of a billion dollar annual loss for BA.

It was in this gloomy environment that Rod Eddington kept his pre-arranged appointment to talk about Australia. The setting was BA's headquarters at Waterside, just outside Heathrow airport, a new complex designed to feel more like a modern village than a corporate tower, with lots of walkways, coffee shops, and open space. Even the executive level is in the same vein — light, spacious, airy and with furniture that wouldn't look too out of place in a patio-lounge.

The space fits Rod Eddington's own style perfectly. Across a low, glass-topped table he is in shirtsleeves, sipping coffee and talking about Australia's future with infectious enthusiasm.

We are running late — courtesy of the only cab driver operating out of Heathrow who doesn't know the BA headquarters — and so Eddington is obliged to keep the conversation moving, with one eye surreptitiously on the clock. He does so with remarkable good grace, considering he has another meeting to follow and that is in Westminster a good 45 minutes drive away — or more, depending on London's peak hour traffic.

Despite these pressures he talks fluently and precisely. The thoughts are carefully constructed but delivered with an easy eloquence. Just occasionally there are distant echoes of the former university lecturer in the style, but these are overshadowed by a general sense of openness.

Rod Eddington has a theory that Australians have developed their own management style, one that combines easy informality with high efficiency. If so, he is an archetypal example. At the end of the meeting he grabs his jacket and asks: 'Where are you heading now? Need a lift?' The tone and the gesture are unequivocally Australian.

Those who work with him say the gesture is characteristic in another way: despite all the pressures on him he is remarkably considerate. He has a young family of his own, for example, and not only does he try to avoid late night and weekend appointments himself, but makes a real effort not to inflict them needlessly on his staff. There's no question he comes across to just about everyone who has had dealings with him as a remarkably balanced individual.

The challenge is to get closer to Asia

The view I can offer of Australia is that of someone who has spent most of his working life outside Australia, but on the other hand, the only passport I have is an Australian passport, so I regard myself as an Australian.

When I think of Australia, I'm conscious first of the opportunities there — which come in part from the wonderful place it is to live; terrific environment, wonderful climate, a sort of an outdoorsy world, a can-do spirit.

For me, one of the great things about the 2000 Olympics in Sydney was that the Sydneysiders in particular and Australians in general, demonstrated they could take up one of the greatest challenges going, which is to successfully stage an Olympic Games with all the issues that surround it — facilities and services for the athletes, the administrators, and the spectators; transport, communications, security — in a whole range of sporting events which go on literally for weeks.

Better still they did it with an amazing sureness of touch, in a wonderfully relaxed sort of way. Australians kept the manner informal, but everything worked; it was the perfect mix. For me living in England, it was just Australia at its best. To be frank, the Australians did a much better job of the Sydney Olympics than the Americans did of the Atlanta Olympics in 1996 — and traditionally the Americans do these things better than anybody else.

That showed me what Australia was capable of doing. It was a fantastic achievement.

But when we look at where Australia goes from here, it is impossible to ignore geography. Australia's isolation is in part its strength; its pristineness and the sort of opportunity it offers, all flow from that isolation. But that is also its weakness. It's a long way away from many of its major markets, even in a shrinking world. We live in a world where air travel and telecommunications make our world smaller, but notwithstanding that, Australia is still a long way away from the world's key centres in the US, Europe and even Asia.

Compounding that, it is a relatively small domestic market: only 20 million or so people, very thinly spread around a big country. Actually most people live in Brisbane, Sydney, Melbourne, Adelaide, Perth, but even those places are still a long, long way from one another, so it is not merely a small market but a series of even smaller markets widely separated from each other. It's a large country with all the distributional challenges that flow from that, but with a small market. So, for a lot of industries Australia is not a high priority.

That's a challenge for Australia when it comes to attracting new investment. There have been various issues raised over the years — forgetting about the issues of distance and size I've just talked about — but issues as to whether things like the taxation regime and our foreign investment rules make Australia an attractive place to invest. In truth, I think governments of both persuasions in Australia, whether they're Liberal or Labor, recognise the need to create an environment inside Australia which is seen as more welcoming for foreign investment.

Because our own capital markets are fairly limited?

Absolutely — and it's one of the reasons the Australian dollar is relatively weak.

So, I'm conscious of the challenges for big foreign entities doing business in Australia. Having said that, both in my time at Cathay Pacific and in my time at BA, Australia was an important part. Cathay flew, and still flies to Cairns, Brisbane, Sydney, Melbourne, Adelaide, Perth. And British Airways flies to Sydney and Melbourne and has a joint venture with Qantas to serve the other major cities in Australia, so I've worked for companies that have made a commitment to Australia and the Australian market. But I'm conscious of the challenges involved.

I've long believed that to be a successful economy — and a successful community — you need what I would call high-quality infrastructure, both hard and soft. What do I mean by soft infrastructure? The rule of law, a legitimate judiciary, sensible political processes, English as a spoken language. Australia has got all of those things.

What do I mean by hard? Road, rail, ports, airports, the telecommunications infrastructure. By and large I think Australia does pretty well at those things — the hard infrastructure — too. Things like our telcos, our airlines, and our airports and our road and rail system are increasingly competitive in a global sense. When you're as isolated as Australia, you need all those things to work well because otherwise people just won't touch you. We've got to make sure our infrastructure, hard and soft, is top quality and that it stays top quality — and I think Australia does pretty well there.

I think there's a real role for Sydney as a global financial centre, particularly as Tokyo has struggled in recent years for a whole series of reasons. Given time zones, New York, London and Sydney, give you good global coverage, so it doesn't surprise me that Sydney is increasingly seen as an important global financial centre. Not just the financial centre of Australia, but a global financial centre.

The real question for the Australian economy is that, given that traditionally we've been seen as, sort of Europe's farm and Asia's mine, how do we move beyond that without replacing them — because agriculture and resources are, and in my view always will be, important parts of the Australian trade picture. How do we grow our services sector?

Tourism is increasingly important — well, just not increasingly; it is already massively important. I think tourism now employs one in nine Australians directly or indirectly.

Do you see Asian tourism being a growth area?

Oh yes, I have no doubt. There is really only one mature Asian outbound market at the moment; that's Japan. Maybe Hong Kong and Singapore are in there too, but there are a lot of other big countries in Asia, where people are only just beginning to travel overseas in any sort of numbers. And although Asians traditionally when they first travel overseas tend to go to other parts of Asia, as they become more confident tourists, they pretty quickly broaden their reach and they go to other parts of the world. And there's no doubt that many more people in Asia and in Europe and in North America will come to visit Australia. So I see tourism as being the major earner of foreign currency for Australia. I believe it is that already and I have no doubt that it will continue to be that. Not only is international tourism important, but domestic tourism as well. We Australians are great travellers within our own country, and that's a good thing.

Then you've got things like financial services. As I have said, I think Sydney can position itself as a global trading centre, up there with New York and London, and that should be a legitimate aspiration. That will be another string to Australia's economic bow.

But these other aspirations shouldn't mean trying to downplay agriculture and resources.

These collectively still provide a very large part of our overseas earnings. They are important for us domestically and internationally and they provide welcome buffers at important times for us. But we need to develop other fields as well and I think Australia's done a pretty good job of that in recent times; and not just with tourism, although that is a real success story.

Australian manufacturing tends to get heavily discounted in the overall scheme of things, again because we've got such a tiny domestic market. But there are some areas where we do produce world-class manufactured goods. Some of the ships and catamarans, the ferries that we make for example, in places like Tasmania and Western Australia are world class. Our wine exports — maybe that's a bit more in the agricultural products sector, but if you walk through a supermarket here in London you'll see 30 different Australian wines on the shelves, and if you walk into a fine wine shop, you'll see 30 more premium Australian wines on the shelves.

So, I think Australia's already broadening its expertise and its standing in the global trading world. Education's huge; hugely important domestically in Australia of course as a basis for other industries, but also as an industry in its own right.

An Australian education is increasingly seen in Asia as an education that's on a par with an American or a British education. And a lot cheaper, because of where the Aussie dollar is. We have excellent institutions, schools and universities, technical colleges.

When I worked at Cathay Pacific, all Cathay's young pilots were — are — trained in Australia at Parafield just out of Adelaide where there's a flying college. You know that's an example of how Australia is tapping the education market in a specialised and lucrative area. The Australian education system's a very good one and already an important exporter. I was an undergraduate in the University of Western Australia. There were some overseas students there in my day but there are many, many, more now, not just from places like Hong Kong or Singapore, or Malaysia and Indonesia — which I guess have more traditionally looked to Australia — but from India and further afield.

I think Australia now has a much broader sweep of things to offer the world. My instincts are that we haven't always had enough confidence in what we do and how we do it, and what we produce. We've had plenty of confidence in our sporting teams' ability to do well internationally, whether it was our tennis players — the Rod Lavers, John Newcombes and Lleyton Hewitts of this world — or whether it was our cricket team, or our rugby union team, or our rugby league team, or our women's hockey team or whatever. But we haven't necessarily had the same confidence in our ability to compete in a global trading sense. My instincts are that we're getting some confidence in that area too — and I think the success of people like Rupert Murdoch and Geoffrey Bible in truly global industries shows that Australians can make it anywhere, not just on the sporting field.

When you look at Murdoch, Bible and others involved in this project like Jac Nasser and Leigh Clifford and Bob May, it speaks to the quality of our education system. It speaks to the quality of life in Australia that it produces people who are rounded, sensible individuals who can go off to other parts of the world and make a go of it. It speaks to the whole social environment in Australia that gives young people the confidence to grow and develop and then go off and explore the world without being unnecessarily constrained by the fear that life's going to be different overseas. That speaks to the Australian way of life, not just to the quality of education systems.

You find young Australians all over the world. By the way, it's traditionally one of the things the Brits have been pretty good at too. You know, they've packed their bags and gone, whether it was in the old days going to India, or Burma, or America, or Australia — and young Brits still do today. Aussies are the same and they generally make a go of it. They make it their business to get on with people around them.

So I think that while we are no longer surprised with the success of our sports men and women overseas, we shouldn't be surprised at the success of business people living overseas either. We've always accepted that we've had some fine international artists — Dame Joan Sutherland, people like that who've been good internationally at what they do.

Let's come back to Australia wine, because that offers a good parallel. There was a time when Australian wine was viewed overseas as well, cheap plonk really. Now everyone accepts that Australia makes world-class wines: a terrific fruit and really well-made wines that have their own distinctive style. For me that's a neat encapsulation of the way in which Australia has been able to go upmarket, if I can use that expression; to compete at higher levels. Maybe the Sydney Olympics was the ultimate achievement in that regard. We showed we could do it on a big scale there.

Back in 1956 the Melbourne games were very successful too — I think they were called the 'friendly games'. But impressive though that achievement was, Sydney was perhaps better because back in 1956 the demands were lower; people's expectations were less. In 2000 the challenges were seen as formidable, particularly given the experience of Atlanta in 1996. The success of the Sydney Olympics was astonishingly broad — it was not just the facilities and the administration, but also the volunteers, the way in which they just transformed the city. The expectations of visitors are far higher today too — the standards they expect from hotels, restaurants, of service generally.

All that gave us a benchmark. The challenge now — whether we are making cars or wine or doing business overseas — the challenge is showing that the Olympics weren't a one-off; that in fact that's the way things now are in Australia. We do quality work.

The games had a particular Australian style that was informal, but informality was no indicator of slap-dash; it wasn't sloppy. It wasn't 49 per cent or 51 per cent will be good enough; we were going to make sure things worked properly first time and every time. To do that in the best Australian way — relaxed and informal but still efficient — that's a difficult balance to pull off. Sydney and Australia showed the world that it can be done.

Is that an emerging Australian management style?

It is a good management style. You can't scream and jump up and down and thump the desk. You've got to try and bring people with you in business. You've got to know your business, and know your people, but you've got to bring them with you — that's an important part of leadership whether it's in business, on the sporting field, or in public life.

All the people I have spoken to on this project have been great communicators. It is a common characteristic.

You have to be. You can't do your job unless you can communicate well, whether it's talking to an individual one on one, standing up in front of two hundred staff, or standing up in front of a thousand customers. You've got to be able to communicate; you've got to know where they're coming from, what the issues are. You've got to love what you do and you've got to like the people you work with. If you do all those things, your job's much easier.

Having worked in Asia, is there a cultural barrier to Australians being fully accepted in Asia?

I don't believe so. It's been my experience — and I've worked in Korea, Hong Kong and Japan, and I've travelled extensively elsewhere in Asia — that there is no barrier to Australians working in Asia, and being accepted there and doing business there, provided they take the time and effort to understand. For me it was never an effort because it was always great fun, to understand the local people, their culture, their food, their way of doing things. I genuinely enjoyed living in those places in Asia. So for me learning something about the people and the way they do things was just part and parcel of being there.

I don't sense any hostility towards Australians in general, in a collective sense. That doesn't mean to say there haven't been Australians who've done some pretty silly things, but in a collective sense, no. My sense is that Australia is entirely part of Asia economically, that our economies are absolutely intertwined. Coal, natural gas, minerals, farm products, food, and services, tourism particularly — our economies are entirely intertwined.

So Australia is at the heart of Asia economically. It is on the edge of Asia geographically and we're some further distance away from Asia culturally. Not nearly as far away from Asia culturally as we used to be, because there are many people of Asian descent now living in Australia. And many young and older Australians now travel quite extensively in Asia, whereas thirty or forty years ago they never did.

The great challenge for us as Australians is to get as close to Asia culturally as we are economically. We can do that without giving up our Australian-ness: we should never give that up, but we can know and understand the various Asian cultures better.

I don't want Australians to ever be anything other than Australians and many of my Asian friends in Australia are proud to be Australians, albeit that they're equally proud of their Asian links, but they're proud to be Australians.

I don't think we should set about trying to blindly mimic Asia. And the Asians themselves don't do it. The Chinese and the Chinese in Taiwan recognise they're very different to the Thais; the Indonesians recognise they're very different to the Japanese, the Koreans recognise that they're very different to the Singaporeans, that's fine.

So for me it's about saying, we as Australians have confidence in the way we are Australian. We're delighted to be part of Asia in the way which I've described. We need the confidence to be Australian on the one hand and to enjoy and relish and build our Asian links on the other. That is entirely do-able.

CHAPTER NINE

Looking for consensus

What messages are there for Australia in these views of six remarkable individuals?

Not surprisingly, given their widely different backgrounds and commercial interests, there is no perfect consensus among the six leaders, but reading their views in the preceding chapters, it becomes abundantly clear that on one issue they are agreed: change is inevitable. The world is changing around us and we must adapt to it.

Four changes are consistently discussed:

- technological change
- the resultant change in the nature of wealth creation, leading to a refocus on human capital rather than physical capital
- the breaking down of international barriers to trade and investment
- the emergence of Asia as an economic and political power centre.

Although the views of each of the six are detailed separately in earlier chapters, it is worth exploring the surprising degree of consensus — or at least synchronicity — of views on those issues.

The changes created by technology are profound. Not merely has it changed the nature of employment (a mere fraction of the population is now required to produce the necessities of life, as

Lord May notes), but it has changed the nature of wealth creation. As Murdoch observes, a spidery imprint on a chip of silica — whose physical value can be costed in cents — can now create vastly more wealth than a farm, a factory or a mine.

That has also changed the nature of capital. Human capital is tending to replace physical capital as the yardstick for a nation's wealth. Human capital includes two elements — numbers of people and their education levels and hence their capacity for innovation. Both get considerable attention across the interviews.

On the question of numbers, Murdoch, Bible and Nasser all identify a policy of incerased immigration as a key priority for Australia. The years both Nasser and Bible have spent in the USA have led them (independently: they've had few opportunities to talk together) to the view that an open-armed approach to immigration has created much of the vitality that has made the US economy the engine of the world. Each of them also looks back to the Australia of their youth when more than a million migrants poured into Australia from war-ravaged Europe (and elsewhere) and provided a massive economic, intellectual and cultural stimulus. A later generation of migrants, many from Indo-China, has had a similar impact and given us better links and a better understanding with Asia, says Rod Eddington.

In his office in London, Leigh Clifford volunteers similar thoughts. He and a number of senior business colleagues have for some years been seeking to encourage an accelerated immigration program.

But if immigration is the key to increasing the volume of our human capital, education is the key to improving its quality — with Rupert Murdoch urging that we concentrate on education 'even to the extent of starving other services.'

There is surprising consensus that the quality of the current Australian education system is broadly comparable with other developed nations. There is equal agreement, however, that we must build further on that base — for high-quality education is increasingly a key to national competitiveness. Not just education, but science — and equally important, the commercialisation of scientific research, for this is the key to creating the new high-value industries that we will increasingly need.

The two most comprehensive proposals for addressing this come from Rupert Murdoch and Robert May and each proposal reflects the character of its author.

Murdoch's proposal is, like many of his business strategies, bold and decisive, cutting directly to the chase even at the risk of offending the existing educational and scientific establishment. His approach might be defined as a call to identify the goal and take the shortest route to it — find the best researchers in some field, bring them to an Australian institution (whatever the price) and the best students will follow. In his opinion, such a course would create a centre of excellence, replicating for some Australian state what Stanford University did for California when it spawned Silicon Valley.

Lord May, as befits an eminent scientist and environmentalist, has conducted extensive research and offers a more evolutionary approach to enhancing and adapting the current institutions to create overall competence. However, both ultimately seek the same goal: fostering and harnessing scientific talent to create economic and social value.

These two areas — immigration and education — quickly emerge as cornerstones of any blueprint the group might draw up for protecting Australia's future.

There is also considerable consensus that a vision for Australia must also incorporate another crucial reality: globalisation.

Several of the leaders try to avoid the term globalisation, because it has come to carry a whole load of emotional baggage; more commonly they use terms like 'trade liberalisation' or 'reduction of barriers to trade and investment'. Regardless of the terminology, there is absolute agreement among the five business figures (Lord May does not venture into the topic, preferring to concentrate on his specialty areas of science and education) that globalisation is a fact of life. It is happening; it will not go away. The only issue, they say, is how we adapt to meet it.

They do not see globalisation as something driven by US big business to the disadvantage of poorer nations. It is something that is occurring because all parties want it. Developing nations are as anxious to get access to the huge, affluent markets of North America and Europe as Western nations are to access the markets of the poorer nations. And everybody wants access to technology and capital.

Progress in trade liberalisation may be uneven, with many developed countries anxious — for domestic political reasons — to shield their farmers from the trend, but the five business leaders all agree that the benefits of freer commerce are such that pressures will continue to lower barriers everywhere — despite what Leigh Clifford calls 'Canute-like efforts' by some people to stop it.

These moves to freer trade, says Jac Nasser, are driven by the costly lessons of an earlier phase of protective economic nationalism and by the prosperity that has flowed from the creation of free trade groups like the European Union. They are also accelerated by the growth of global communications which makes doing business across national boundaries infinitely easier (and even rendering national boundaries less relevant).

Nasser's historical explanation is so succinct and so persuasive that one is forced to ask the next question: if globalisation is both inevitable and inherently good, why so many protests?

Answers to the question are implicit in the comments of Leigh Clifford, who points out that trade deal protests are occurring not in Mexico, but 'across the border' in the US. Competition means change according to Clifford, and change is often painful.

Separate to this broad question of improving our global trade links (which we are already doing quite successfully) is the question of our relations with Asia. The so-called Asian Meltdown of the 1990s and the prolonged sluggishness of Japan's economy has led to a general view that the 'Asian miracle' is over.

Not so, say the leaders. Rupert Murdoch is in awe of the growth in living standards that China has achieved — and is still achieving. And India, while less spectacular and more uneven in its growth than China, has still come a long way and is creating an affluent middle class of impressive proportions. Other Asian countries are also moving forward and the picture that emerges is of a continent with a massive youthful population hell-bent on improving its living standards.

All the business figures see Asia as a hugely important element in Australia's future; its size and its potential to sharply lift living standards ensure that it will offer massive trade potential.

To understand why the leaders put such emphasis on Asia, you need only look at the figures. In 1988 the developing nations of Asia (that is, excluding Japan and South Korea which were already highly industrialised) together accounted for just 7 per cent of the world's income. Just twelve years later in 2002 they accounted for 22 per cent (see Table 3).

Nor is that trend likely to slacken. Official forecasts (Table 4) show that in 2003 Western Europe is tipped to grow at under 3 per

Table 3: Share of world income (%)

	1998	2002	2010
OECD countries	76	56.5	52.2
Non-OECD Asia (ie without Japan and Korea)	7	22.0	26.2
Latin America	6	8.4	8.4
Russia	4	2.5	2.8
Middle East	3	4.0	4.0
Africa	2	3.2	3.1
Others	2	3.4	3.3

Source: ABARE, Australian Commodities, vol. 9, no. 1, March quarter 2002

cent and the US at 3.8 per cent, while China is forecast to expand at 7.7 per cent, India 5 per cent and South-East Asia 4.3 per cent.

Rod Eddington, who has spent sixteen years living and working in Asia — and running a major business there — sees building closer links with Asia as both Australia's greatest opportunity and greatest challenge.

But while all the business leaders are familiar with these figures, they are also global thinkers. Even as they talk of the potential of Asia, they also urge that Australia push forward with its claim to join the North American Free Trade Agreement and hopefully, extend those links eventually to all the Americas.

And to look elsewhere too. To think globally is to recognise that the whole world offers opportunities. And those opportunities will be wherever enterprising Australians can find them.

This then is the picture that emerges from the six leaders. We are entering a world where trade and investment barriers are falling and communications are improving; where science and technology

Table 4: Forecast economic growth — % change on previous period.

	2000	2001	2002	2003	2004	2005	2006	2007
OECD	3.6	1.2	0.7	3.0	3.1	2.8	2.7	2.7
United States	4.1	1.1	0.5	3.8	3.8	3.5	3.3	3.3
Japan	2.4	-0.5	-1.5	0.5	0.5	0.5	0.5	0.5
Germany	3.0	0.6	0. 7	2.6	2.7	2.5	2.5	2.5
France	3.4	1.9	1.3	3.0	3.0	2.7	2.7	2.7
United Kingdom	3.1	2.2	1.8	2.5	2.8	2.5	2.5	2.5
Italy	2.9	1.8	1.1	2.5	2.7	2.5	2.5	2.5
Korea (Republic of)	8.8	2.9	3.5	5.5	6.0	5.5	5.0	5.0
New Zealand	3.8	2.3	2.0	3.2	3.5	3.5	3.0	3.0
Developing countries:								
South-East Asia (Indonesia, Malaysia, Philippines, Singapore and Thailand)	6.0	1.2	2.4	4.3	5.0	4.7	4.7	4.7
China (incl. Hong Kong)	8.0	7.3	7.0	7.7	7.5	7.5	7.5	8.0
Chinese Taipei	6.0	-2.2	2.0	3.5	5.0	4.5	4.0	4.0
India	5.2	4.0	4.0	5.0	5.5	5.0	5.0	5.0
Latin America	4.2	1.5	0.7	3.0	4.0	3.8	3.5	3.5
Middle East	6.0	4.0	3.5	4.0	4.0	3.5	3.5	3.5
Russian Federation	8.3	5.0	4.0	4.5	4.5	4.0	4.0	4.0
Ukraine	5.8	7.0	4.0	5.0	5.0	4.0	4.0	4.0
Eastern Europe	3.8	2.0	3.0	4.0	4.0	4.0	4.0	4.0

Source: ABARE, Australian Commodities, vol. 9, no. 1, March quarter 2002 can transform old notions of wealth creation; where people and knowledge become more important than physical assets; where despite the awesome power of the US economy, the most dramatic growth is likely to occur in Asia.

It is a world in which, if we are to maintain high living standards, we will need to be in the upper rung of international science, where we will need to move into new knowledge based industries to generate growth and need to improve efficiency in existing industries to hold our place. It is a world in which we will need to become comfortable with other cultures in order to be a global trading nation and yet still maintain our own identity and our own values — for both these things serve us well.

How well equipped are we in Australia to compete in such a world?

The answers are, on balance, optimistic. We certainly carry a few handicaps — size and isolation still ranking high among them — but we also have some real assets. Notwithstanding those assets, and the positive changes we have already made, all of the leaders see us needing further change and further hard decisions if we are to prosper.

Population size will certainly be one of those decisions As Rod Eddington observes, Australia is not just a relatively small market that is remote from the world's major markets — it is more properly a series of even smaller markets scattered across a huge continent. Or, as Geoff Bible puts it, a country with all the distribution challenges of the US without the market size to make it worthwhile.

This poses severe challenges for mass manufacturing.

Smallness and remoteness also limit our ability to influence the world. Rupert Murdoch says that he's often asked what people in the US think about Australia. The answer, he says, is 'They don't think about us much . . . we're not on their minds.'

This indifference has consequences beyond a mere bruising of our national ego; it limits our negotiating capacity. Murdoch argues that Australian membership of NAFTA (the North American Free Trade Agreement), which Australia seeks, would be beneficial and is certainly possible. The problem is not the threat we would pose to some sections of US agriculture; that could be resolved with a few special conditions. The challenge is to get the collective attention of the various people in Washington long enough to negotiate our way through these issues.

Offsetting these handicaps, however, Australia has some impressive assets that have underpinned our economic success for some years now. It comes as a surprise to discover that these include our garrulous politicians, earnest public servants, grumbling teachers, pompous judges and even our hard-hearted tax collectors. Stable democracy, the rule of law, a relatively uncorrupted public service and a good education system emerge as vital economic assets. (In spelling out our assets the six leaders may also unwittingly explain why the problems of the Third World are so intransigent; without these social and institutional assets they struggle to attract investment capital).

Because the interviewees were selected for their success in business and science, the focus of the discussions was initially expected to be more economic than social, but in the minds of these international figures the distinction is less clear. 'You cannot have a vibrant healthy country if you don't have vibrant enterprises,' says Jac Nasser. 'On the other hand I don't think you can have the reverse either. They go together.'

Scientists too, it seems, need a degree of social consensus. Lord

May notes that much science today is on the fringes of knowledge; venturing into areas where issues of ethics and risk are no longer clear-cut. Guidelines are needed. He urges open debate and transparent decision-making. Bringing into these discussions people with other agendas — both philosophical and material — can be tedious and time consuming, he says, but is ultimately far preferable to decision-making by presumed specialists behind closed doors.

This raises wider questions which the leaders were willing to address. The respective roles of governments and markets in guiding Australia through these changes; the relationship between business and the community and the role of philanthropy, both corporate and private in filling the gaps left by increasingly strained government budgets.

The feeling that a successful economy and a successful society are interdependent recurs several times.

One might have expected hard-nosed business leaders to talk of Australia's competitiveness in terms of tax rates and industrial awards, just as one might have expected Lord May to push for massive funding injections as the central plank of a science policy. In truth, these expressions of self-interest rarely emerged as central issues. Rather it is Rupert Murdoch, the professed advocate of low tax and small government, who calls for massive public investment in science and education and it is Lord May, academic and environmentalist, who talks of the role of entrepreneurial academics in developing science-based industry.

This willingness of all six participants to take a broader view suggests that they not only have the intellectual sweep one expects of global leaders but that they can put the long-term future of Australia ahead of any sectional interests.

CHAPTER TEN

Revolutionary Australia and the way forward

One of the more pleasant surprises to emerge from the six discussions is the discovery that Australia has already moved part of the way along the paths outlined by the participants.

Indeed, when you look at the changes to which the interviewees refer — changes in immigration patterns, in tariffs, the floated dollar, workplace reform and relations with Asia — it comes as almost a shock to realise that Australia has in the past few decades undergone something little short of a revolution.

It is a revolution which is not acknowledged in its totality by any of the six; rather, it is revealed piecemeal in casual references to changes that have occurred. Think of Jac Nasser talking of a tax system that once had a reputation for being inflexible and not very responsive. 'I don't see that any more,' he says. Or industrial relations and Geoff Bible recalling that a couple of decades ago Philip Morris had to deal with nine different unions at a single plant in Australia — with all the resultant problems of demarcation disputes and different award conditions. Now he says there is only one. And Leigh Clifford, talking on our evolving attitudes to foreign investment, remarking that Australia wouldn't want to handicap itself by going back to some of the policies of twenty years ago. Or of Geoff Bible attributing Australia's ability to survive the Asian Meltdown of the later-1990s to the progressive devaluation of theAustralian dollar, a process much eased by the decision taken a few years earlier to end fixed exchange rates and float the currency.

These are all quite remarkable changes.

Industry gets some credit too. Rod Eddington notes that despite all the difficulties of remoteness and a small domestic market, there are Australian manufacturers who are pushing out and finding global export markets — for wines, specialist ships, computer services and footwear, to name just some. Jac Nasser makes the same observation, citing cars and car components and even biomedical products.

Those quoted examples are fully supported by official statistics. Reserve Bank of Australia figures show that in 2001 exports of motor vehicles totalled 129 000, worth more than A$4 billion, (and with subsequent US contracts are now likely to head towards A$5 billion a year). In the same year wine and beverage sales reached $2 billion; pharmaceuticals A$1.8 billion and computer services A$750 million.

Of all the changes though, the one that excites most admiration has been our ability to adjust to the quite sweeping changes in the make-up of our population over the past 35 years. Notwithstanding some of the tensions that have emerged in Australia in recent years, those who have lived in the US and UK still comment on the relative harmony of the change.

'I can't think of any other country that could have made that change so harmoniously — not even the US, as good as it is at assimilating new cultures and new ideas. I think Australia is remarkable,' says Jac Nasser.

Bible and Murdoch both describe the broadening of our migrant base as 'terrific' and Rod Eddington, while urging greater progress in building cultural bridges with Asia, still acknowledges that we have come a long way.

(All were talking in general terms, but the scale of that change in our immigration policy is clear from ABS figures. Of the 20 020 permanent settler arrivals in the first quarter of 2002, 9240 were from Asia and the Middle East compared with a total of 3820 from Britain, Europe and the former Soviet Union and 3880 from New Zealand and the Pacific.

In many cases the recognition of what has been done was merely a precursor to outlining greater changes that are still required. Nonetheless, all those brief acknowledgements add up to a picture of a nation that has made quite extraordinary changes in little more than twenty years. It paints us as an adaptable society and one with good reason to believe we can make the further adjustments needed to equip us for a changing world.

Jac Nasser and Rod Eddington both see this adaptability as a core strength and one of the reasons to be optimistic about Australia's future. Nasser sees it as the great hope for Australian industry; a nimbleness that will enable us to find niche markets in a globalised world economy. Eddington sees the ability of young Australians to get on with people and to accept and understand other cultures without surrendering our own values as a key to finding our place in Asia, the great growth centre of the twenty-first century.

That does not mean, however, that the changes were pain-free — or will be pain-free in future. Far from it: the restructuring of industries to make them competitive cost many people their jobs; some when they were at an age when re-employment in other fields was difficult. Leigh Clifford witnessed such changes and sympathises. Nonetheless, he says the costs of not changing, of remaining uncompetitive, would have been much higher. Having undergone the pain of one round of change there is a natural human tendency to want to call for a pause, but that pause may not be a luxury we are granted. Clifford suggests that the pace of change is more likely to quicken than slow.

Nonetheless, Australia has shown a remarkable capacity for adaptation and none of the changes ahead may be so fundamental as those we have undergone in the past few decades, moving from a protected economy to an open, outward-looking one; from an Anglo-European nation to one which now embraces migrants from all continents.

The challenges ahead may be great, but they may be no greater than those we have overcome and not a few of our business leaders believe that the quiet revolution we have undergone is proof of our capacity to recognise realities and adapt to them.

CHAPTER ELEVEN

So where do we go from here?

Six Australians who have made their mark at the highest levels have offered their views on how they see Australia's future. They talk of the forces operating on us and suggest responses we might make but, conscious that they now spend much of their time abroad, none is confident or arrogant enough to say: 'This is what Australia must do.'

They have sketched us a map of the future, but they make it clear that ultimately it is Australians and their elected leaders who will decide which road we will take.

So what are the prospects of us seizing the opportunities they outline and avoiding the pitfalls? Surprisingly good.

Australians traditionally do not speak fondly of their politicians. Our cynicism toward them is often regarded — perhaps with some justification — as a healthy protection against the hazards of charismatic leaders and ideological extremism and in general we prefer to view our leaders through the eyes of cartoonists rather than acolytes.

Yet history may judge Australia's leaders of the past twenty years a little more kindly than have their contemporary caricaturists. If the perspectives offered in this book prove accurate, then it will be said that Prime Ministers Hawke, Keating and Howard were remarkably prescient in pushing through the enormous structural changes that they made; the floating of the dollar, the progressive reduction of tariffs, tax reforms, the engagement with Asia, the push for other bilateral trade agreements, the broadening of our immigrant base, the opening of business to competition and the associated workplace changes will all be seen to have provided a valuable foundation.

Because these changes carried few immediate political benefits, and often considerable costs (and in the case of the Labor leaders evoked hostility from their core constituency) those three may even earn that accolade — so rarely bestowed on Australian leaders — of being called statesmen.

We should not be shy of acknowledging this, for we may need even greater political courage from our next generation of leaders.

In a society where an ageing population will produce ever-growing pressure for greater spending on health services and welfare, it will take a leader with considerable courage to divert scarce resources to the expansion of scientific research, education and training. Businesses, faced with the constant pressures of competition, will need to still incur the costs of up-skilling, retraining and research and development. Many will also need to divert resources to the development of overseas markets, an investment that frequently takes huge perseverance to produce dividends, but which will be vital to our national survival.

The demands will come not only on our leaders, but on us all. We may be forced to review the appropriateness of our traditional attitudes in many areas. What provides cause for optimism is that we have already shown a remarkable capacity to adapt to changing needs.

If we look at the views of the six leaders who participated here — and who bring an impressive range of perspectives to bear — four areas present themselves as imperative to our future: science and education, immigration, greater international engagement and a greater enlistment of corporate and personal philanthropy.

It is easy to pay lip service to these views, but much harder to make the commitments that are inherent in them. We may have to make some hard choices. Let's consider the options

Science, technology and education

Two of the participants — Rupert Murdoch and Lord May — offer specific formulae for boosting our competence. The two views are not mutually exclusive, but they do take very different approaches: Murdoch's offering to swiftly create global excellence in specific areas and May's aiming to create broad-based competitiveness and relevance across a wide range of disciplines. Each would require changes in the way we currently do things.

Murdoch's would require dramatic change; offering big name researchers pop-star incomes to come to Australia would revolutionise the whole approach to academic salaries. However, the scenario Murdoch paints, of creating a technology–industry nexus like that between Stanford University and Silicon Valley is so tantalising that it is hard to dismiss. One wonders whether it would not be a worthy task for some large corporation or industry grouping, perhaps with State government backing. In providing private funding, such a group would earn the right to both direct it to a specific area of research and to supplement official university salaries in any manner they saw fit. That would not ensure such research was free of criticism from the rest of the academic community, but it would make it possible.

The level of funding required — and it would need to be sustained for perhaps a decade to bear real fruit — is also such that only a handful of Australian businesses could contemplate it. Perhaps it might require a cooperative venture; for example the major banks, the major resource companies or the motor industry. It may take an enterprising State government to pull it together, but when the prize is a possible world-class centre of knowledge-based industry, it may be worth the effort.

This scenario does not absolve government of the responsibility for addressing the other half of Murdoch's vision, that of boosting education spending 'even to the point of starving other services.' Given the power of other pressure groups, that would take considerable political courage and is likely to eventuate only if there is wide (and articulated) public support. If we want it to happen, we must tell our leaders.

Lord May's proposals are aimed at creating across-the-board scientific progress and have a huge advantage in that many of his suggestions are already being adopted by the UK, which means implementation issues are in the process of being addressed. One of the most pressing (and perhaps easiest) issues to address would seem to be the creation of a fund to support early research into commercialisation prospects for scientific advances. As Lord May has noted, this is commonly a bottleneck; it is difficult to attract commercial investors until the groundwork has been done, but mechanisms to fund it are almost non-existent.

Though he is refreshing in not letting his proposals become simply yet another plea for greater government funding as a universal panacea — and in fact puts considerable effort into the question of how to get better results from existing funds allocation — Lord May's views do provide a persuasive argument for more support from government. He accepts that a nation of Australia's size will always have to adapt or adopt a high proportion of its technology, but argues that even this is possible only if we have enough high-class scientists to earn a place in the main game. To do that you have to bring something to the table; to make a contribution to the available store of knowledge. If we cannot do that we will fall behind, not only because we do not develop our own technology, but because we will be too slow in comprehending the opportunities or the consequences of other developments. It is also necessary just to provide opportunity for bright young Australians.

That view is persuasive grounds for diverting more money to research.

It is not, alas, so simple: an equally persuasive case can be made that more money is also needed for all the teaching arms — including both TAFE and postgraduate university education. It is now widely argued that formal education is no longer something you receive in a single dose in your youth, but will increasingly be a lifelong process. People will need specific training at various points in their lives to equip them for promotion or career changes or for advances in technology (a theory known as 'just-in-time' education). Jac Nasser notes that some of the most effective executives at Ford had done apprenticeships then later went on to do degrees, postgraduate courses and even doctorates. There is a need for increased services in this area.

On-line education is also an area of increasing relevance. Rod Eddington and Lord May both note that it has the potential to increase Australia's education exports, but also to bring our universities into direct competition with prestigious international institutions. We need to allocate sufficient funds to ensure we are not left behind in developing the skills and technologies to successfully compete in the on-line education marketplace.

For Australia these proposals bring not only the obvious

pressure for increased funding for education overall, but inevitable debate about how and where that funding will be applied: to broad-based general education, to postgraduate studies, technical and vocational training or to high level research? Or to commercialisation of that research?

In a world where resources are always finite this may mean reviewing some traditional and treasured approaches and values, not least of which is the complex question of how much of the cost of education should be borne by the recipient — or by industry. Or the question of whether there is a single funding regime or whether a handful of institutions should be additionally supported to make them world class. There are no easy answers.

The six interviewees in this book have indelibly underscored the crucial role of education and research in determining our future living standards. They have set an agenda for debate, but only the Australian public can have — and resolve — the debates on whether we fund education at the expense of other social needs and where we allocate additional education funding. If we are to seize the opportunities the evolving world presents us, these are debates we have to have.

Immigration

In recent years the question of the treatment of illegal arrivals on our shores has tended to hugely overshadow the larger issues of the scale and scope of our total immigration policy. However, concern about low childbirth rates and the greying of Australia are again beginning to refocus debate on what is a desirable population level — a decision that has environmental as well as economic considerations.

Four of the six participants in this book — Murdoch, Clifford, Bible and Nasser — spontaneously raise immigration as one of the critical factors affecting our future. Each favours a sustained immigration program.

Their arguments are essentially two-pronged: that our population size (and its fragmentation over a large continent) limits our capacity to sustain some economic activities and that migrants bring energy and vibrancy. One gets the impression they rate the latter more highly. Rod Eddington adds a third argument that the influx of Asian migrants and their progressive acceptance into mainstream society has broken down some of our cultural isolation from Asia and will in time help forge wider economic and social links.

All five (Lord May did not touch on the issue) talked approvingly of the way in which Australia has been able to broaden its cultural mix if not without tensions, at least without the riots and violence that have occurred elsewhere.

We have done well, but have we done enough? Murdoch, Bible, Clifford and Nasser unashamedly recommend an accelerated immigration program and point to the USA as an example of the economic and intellectual energy that flows from large-scale immigration.

Australia currently maintains a gently rising immigration flow of a little over 100 000 a year. Is that sufficient, too few or too many? The consensus of the business leaders in this book is that it is too few. The current Australian emphasis is on accepting skilled migrants, but the US has been far less discriminating — unskilled migrants, both legal and illegal, make up the majority of its inflows. Does this require a review of our migrant mix or would a more open door stretch Australia's welfare system?

Increasing our international engagement

At an official level in Australia, participation in international trade agreements is no longer an issue. Both major parties have for more than a decade simultaneously pursued the twin paths of multilateral and bilateral agreements to increase Australia's trade access abroad. Both parties have enjoyed some success.

That participation seems likely to continue with the great diplomatic challenge being to negotiate access to North America without prejudicing our relations with Asia. It is not an insurmountable task, for other nations have managed to enjoy relations with more than one trading bloc, but it will require some finesse. Progress in the other great area of frustration — that of overcoming the hypocrisy of developed nations, particularly in Europe, who urge free trade in manufactures while keeping the doors firmly shut to agricultural competition — will be harder and slower.

The opening up of the world to greater trade is, as all the business participants note, highly desirable; the current global push for freer trade is built on the evidence that in general where barriers have fallen, prosperity has risen. Despite the costs involved — for trade agreements, while creating opportunities for some industries, also expose others to competition — Australia has no option but to press forward. We cannot go back to the days when we could harbour inefficient industries behind a tariff wall and rely on primary products for our export revenues. The terms of trade have turned against primary products and they alone can no longer support us; we must increasingly augment them with technology based manufactures and services if we are to maintain our living standards. That is the unmistakable message. The harder task will be to maintain our practical compassion for those hurt by these changes without losing our resolve to press ahead.

The Australian worker: an unsung hero?

In becoming a global competitor Australia may find it has an unexpected asset in the quality of its workforce.

Rod Eddington observes that the success of the Sydney Olympics sent an important message to Australians as well as to the rest of the world: we *can* cut it in the big league; we can match anybody in the world for quality and efficiency when we put our minds to it. It should give us, he says, the confidence to seek world markets in other fields.

The surprise is that we needed such a message. The evidence is all around us that Australians can produce quality products at competitive prices. After all, we export optical equipment and computer services, motor vehicles, footwear and naval patrol boats, all in competition against suppliers from Europe, the US and Asia — not as many of these things as we'd like, of course, but enough to show that there is no inherent barrier to our doing so.

In reviewing our various national assets and liabilities none of the six called into question the quality of our workforce. More commonly it was noted that we had in general an educated workforce 'with a relatively good work ethic.' Even our working hours are no longer considered generous, for much of Western Europe has now matched them.

It was noted earlier that Australia has undergone changes in the past two decades so dramatic that they might well qualify as a quiet revolution. The adjustment we have made to workplace practices and attitudes in order to adapt to a more open economy must rank high in that list of changes. The challenge now is for business to harness these changes to win the export markets on which our future depends. The quality and cost of Australian workers is no longer an excuse for hiding from the challenge.

Philanthropy

Western governments everywhere are under pressure to provide more and better services. Even the growing demands of education outlined above seem dwarfed by the explosive growth of health care costs, driven up by both improving medical technology and the (not unrelated) increases in life expectancy. Health systems everywhere in the Western world are under pressure and an ageing population will inevitably increase costs and reduce the proportion of employed taxpayers. To slow that overall ageing — at least by boosting birthrates to create more younger Australians — there are calls for increased assistance for families.

If an ever-greater proportion of government revenues is needed for these core areas, where does that leave other social programs, like help for the marginalised in our society and assistance for the arts? Must they inevitably suffer? Or can corporate and personal philanthropy pick up part of the tab?

One repeated observation by the interviewees in this book is the degree to which the USA has been able to harness philanthropy to compensate for government funding shortfalls. It is not just a case of philanthropists doing what governments ought to do (though some would argue that is the case in some US welfare programs) but when it comes to things like endowments for universities they outstrip funding sources elsewhere in the world. Lord May, who was head of research at Princeton before being attracted to Oxford, notes that the funding advantage US universities seem to enjoy over many others is due overwhelmingly to the sheer generosity of American endowments.

No Australian university ranks in the world's top 100, but proposals to redress this with government funding run into allegations of elitism. Why should governments give extra support to the universities that are already doing well? Perhaps greater philanthropic contributions are the answer.

A great idea, but how? Clearly tax incentives are one tool, and the Australian Federal Government has already moved in that direction, but it is not the sole answer. There are deeper social forces at work. Jac Nasser notes, for example, that the whole corporate–community relationship is much stronger in the US than in any of the dozen or so other countries where he has been an executive — and that includes Australia.

In the US, he says, companies expect to be part of their local community — not just with cash donations but by having employees involved as volunteers with the support of their employer. Business sees itself as an organic part of the community and the feeling is largely reciprocal. That feeling is far weaker in Australia (and lower still in Europe), he says — and the fault is not entirely with business.

There is a sense that the Australian community is more sceptical of industry involvement in social issues and more cautious about embracing it, unless it means a company simply handing over a cheque and then withdrawing. Anybody who has been involved in public affairs consulting in Australia knows that the first advice to give any company is that if they want to support a good cause, do so for genuine philanthropic motives — don't imagine it will have great public relations benefits. The recognition you receive will be modest compared to the sums you donate.

There is an underlying element of moral virtue in this attitude — that we will not allow companies to buy public goodwill — but it has its costs. It means business can afford to give to worthy causes only that part of their profits which is earmarked for philanthropy. The much greater budgets that are available for corporate reputation and brand recognition don't go to areas where recognition is limited or given reluctantly; after all, no board wants to report to shareholders that its expenditures on PR and marketing achieved little discernible benefit.

Perhaps not unrelated to this is a view from Geoff Bible that many (obviously not all) Americans feel a greater sense of individual responsibility to help the unfortunate. Jac Nasser offers a parallel view when he says that in Australia and Europe there is a feeling that this is a government responsibility not one for individuals or businesses; we tend to feel that our obligations, individual and corporate, are met by our taxes.

As the demands on government revenues grow (and the proportion of the population that is working declines) Australians may choose to review that. We may find there are parts of our society — either in the arts or in welfare — which are not adequately serviced by a government struggling to meet health, welfare and education demands. Greater personal and corporate philanthropy may be required. If that is what we want then we may have to revise our own attitudes — not just our feelings of personal responsibility to give (wherever we are able) but our willingness to give generous recognition to others who do so. There may be a more generous culture of giving when we are willing to give more kudos to those who give.

Our media: A special asset

As we have noted several times in this book, Australia has already made massive changes to adjust to the technological, economic and social transformations that are occurring throughout the world.

That we have become aware of these issues — and have been willing to adjust to them — is in some ways a tribute to our media. Jac Nasser observes that journalism is a field where Australians have been remarkably successful; that you find Australians in key media jobs almost everywhere in the English-speaking world. The world view that this gives our media serves us well.

Change can often mean stress and discomfort, but it also creates opportunity. Our ability to deal with the continuing changes taking place around us, to address the pain and seize the opportunities, is hugely enhanced by having an outward looking media with global perspectives.

It may be also aided by being able to share the perspectives of people who are in their own way shaping this new world and who, by their positions, have access to insights not available to all. That at least was the hope of the six Australians who contributed to this project.

Endnotes

A nation in transition

Page 12: *The End of Certainty: Power, Politics and Business in Australia*, Paul Kelly, Allen & Unwin, 1994.

Page 14: 'In 1907 ... British Empire countries.' *Trade and Excise Review*, Commonwealth Bureau of Census and Statistics, Melbourne, 1907.

Page 15: '...about 66 per cent of Australia's exports...' Overseas Trade 1950–51, Bureau of Census and Statistics, Canberra. Note that this was a stellar year for wool with demand and prices driven up by the Korean War and the sudden need for winter uniforms. Nonetheless overseas trade figures for the year 1947–48 reveal that even in that more normal year wool still accounted for 148 million of our 409 million pounds' worth of exports with wheat and flour and meat and dairy products together accounting for a further 159 million pounds. Australia was overwhelmingly dependent on the export of farm products.

Page 15: '... by 1977–78 was providing just under 10 per cent.' *Exports Australia 1977–78*, ABS, Canberra.

Page 16: 'A side effect ... of traditional attitudes.' *Exports Australia 1977–78*, ABS, Canberra. In 1977–78 Japan took $3.89 billion of our $12.26 billion export total while Britain took only $482 million. Iron and other metallic ores were our biggest earner at $1.6 billion followed by coal at $1.4 billion, grains $1.3 billion and wool $1.19 billion.

Page 17: 'By 2000 Singapore ... a whopping $36,149.' Department of Foreign Affairs and Trade, Canberra. Market Information and Analysis Unit, 2001.

Page 18: 'By 2002 Australia could list ... A$100 million.' ABS Working Paper 2001/10.

Page 19: 'Exports of these products ... to June 2001.' ABS Working Paper 2001/10.

Page 19: *Recollections of a Bleeding Heart: A Portrait of Paul Keating PM*, Don Watson, Knopf 2002.

Revolutionary Australia and the way forward

Page 152: '... 2001 exports of motor vehicles totalled 129 000, worth more than A$4 billion.' Reserve Bank of Australia, 'Trends in Australia's exports', Reserve Bank of Australia Bulletin, April 2002, p.4.

Page 152: '...wine and beverage sales reached $2 billion; pharmaceuticals A$1.8 billion and computer services A$750 million.' ABS Working Paper 2001/10.

Page 153: 'Of the 20 020 permanent settler arrivals in the first quarter of 2002 ...' *Overseas arrivals and departures — January to March 2002*. Doc. 3401.0, ABS, Canberra, p.7.

PHOTOGRAPHY CREDITS

Jac Nasser courtesy Ford Motor Company

Lord May courtesy Oxford University

Rupert Murdoch courtesy News Corporation

Geoff Bible courtesy Altria Corporate Serves Inc.

Leigh Clifford courtesy Rio Tinto Ltd.

Rod Eddington courtesy British Airways

Printed in Dunstable, United Kingdom

88180805R00100